BEATING THE COST OF COOKING

MARY BERRY

Illustrated by Tony Streek

TVTimes FAMILY BOOKS

INDEPENDENT TELEVISION BOOKS LIMITED, LONDON

INDEPENDENT TELEVISION BOOKS LIMITED
247 Tottenham Court Road
London W1P 0AU

© Mary Berry 1975

ISBN: 0 900 72737 3

Printed in Great Britain by
Butler and Tanner Lfd.,
Frome and London

CONTENTS

Introduction 3
1 Your kitchen and your equipment 4
2 Making the most of food 9
3 Starters 22
4 Meat and fish 34
5 One-pot meat cooking 43
6 Cooking with left-overs 52
7 Pasta, cheese and eggs 56
8 Rice and vegetables 64
9 Puddings 69
10 Cakes and biscuits 84

Introduction

Tastes differ. No two families' needs are the same and you may be catering for healthy schoolchildren's appetites, older people's fussy tastes, babies, dedicated slimmers, invalids, or people who just have to watch what they eat. You want to do it economically.

In the chapters that follow I hope to show you what to buy, when to buy it, and how to use it without waste, so that whether you are cooking for one or a dinner party you'll know how to make the best use of your materials, to employ your ingenuity and imagination and to prove to yourself something that the thrifty French housewife has known all along, that the best cooking is not necessarily the most expensive cooking.

Chapter 1
Your kitchen
and your equipment

Many items make the cost of cooking – the actual price of food is only one. But it's the one that gives people the most worry, because it's the most obvious. And when your expenses start to overtake your budget that is the area in which you'll try to make the cuts.

There are nearly always economies that *can* be made in the type of food you buy, and this book will suggest ways and means of doing this, but don't overlook savings in other areas – for example, meals planned so that more than one dish can be cooked at the same time; the nourishing use of left-overs; bulk buying; making use of cheaper ingredients that will achieve the same effect as the more expensive ones. And – by no means the least important but sometimes forgotten – the design of your kitchen, the equipment it contains and the effect of your surroundings on your well-being.

And since it is on this that all other considerations rest, begin in the kitchen and take a look at your comfort.

A contented cook is an imaginative, interested cook. And you have to be interested in what you're doing to cook in the inventive way that's necessary if you're going to save money. Whether you spend a whole morning in the kitchen, or a mere half hour, your surroundings *must* have a big influence on your whole outlook – the way you tackle the job. Take a look around. What colour is your kitchen? (A fresh coat of paint works wonders with the cook's morale.) Is it light? Airy? Have you cut unnecessary work to a minimum? It may be a big, old-fashioned kitchen where the whole of family life goes on, or it may be so small that you can stand in the middle of it and cook a complete dinner without taking more than a single step in any direction. Whatever it is, it can be organised to provide the maximum efficiency. Efficiency saves money.

There are few kitchens that can't be improved with a little thought and planning, and this kind of organisation need not be expensive. The main object is to have everything arranged to make work easier, to cut down on unnecessary effort which is time-wasting and tiring. Often a simple rearrangement of existing equipment is all that's needed.

Eliminate the possibility of accidents. If you accidentally knock a joint of beef to the floor, you can recover and rehabilitate it; with a light and crumbly steak and kidney pie, this is more difficult; with a carefully prepared soup, impossible.

So before you consider the bigger items of equipment, expensive initially but money savers in the end – the home freezer, the electric mixers and blenders, the pressure cooker – look at the kitchen where they're going to be used.

The easiest kitchens to work in are compact, with equipment and foodstuffs ready to hand. Most of them follow a work pattern based on a sequence of operations – storing, preparing, cooking, serving. There are no hard and fast rules; the layout of each area must follow the shape of the whole, but as a general rule it is based on store, sink, preparation area, cooker, refrigerator or freezer; the distance between any of these areas should not be more than 20 feet (6 metres). Layout may be U-shape, L-shape, galley-shape or corridor-shape, or any variation of these according to the space available.

Storage

Accessibility is of prime importance – you shouldn't have to stretch awkwardly to get at anything. Open shelves often work better than cupboards; contents are easier to reach and you can see at a glance what you have.

Cans and packaged goods don't last for ever, so put the new ones at the back and bring forward the ones that have been there longer.

Refrigerators and freezers have now largely taken the place of larders in the modern kitchen, but the cool, well-aired larder is still useful for keeping such things as cheese and eggs, home-bottled fruits, jams and preserves. It need not be as large as it once was; the old-fashioned walk-in larder has given way to the smaller cupboard, which can even be one that hangs on the wall, anywhere with a good circulation of air.

Work surfaces

Aim at having a smooth, continuous surface, as extensive as possible and at a convenient height — awkward heights lead to backache, tiredness and lack of enthusiasm for cooking of any kind. If you can arrange a work top continuous with the sink, so much the better; and have a good heat-proof surface beside the cooker to hold hot pans and dishes.

Work tops can be arranged over cupboards, over a built-in dishwasher or waste disposer, often over the fridge. A good run of cupboards and built-in equipment, with work surfaces above, is the ideal to aim at. I know it can't always be done, and we don't all have a lot of built-in equipment, but a little ingenuity can work wonders.

Flooring

When you have an opportunity of re-covering the floor, do it with a material that is resilient and non-slip — it cuts down fatigue and the possibility of accidents.

Small equipment

Here personal preferences play a big part, but remember that it pays to buy the best you can afford. It's better and more economical in the end to invest in one solid and reliable casserole dish, with or without a non-stick lining, than several flimsy saucepans that consistently burn the soup; you can lose a lot of good material that way.

It's impossible to lay down hard and fast rules and not easy to make detailed lists, because every cook's needs vary according to circumstances and size of family. But everyone will need the following:

Saucepans and frying pans in various sizes	non-stick linings, which are improving all the time, do cut down work
Casseroles	which can be brought straight from oven to table, doubling as cooking and serving dish.
A steamer	
Baking tins	
Kitchen scales	
Good sharp knives and a sharpener	
Spoons	both wooden and metal
Storage equipment, e.g. tins, plastic bags, boxes and jars	
Kitchen paper and foil	keep a good supply, their uses are endless
A mincer	either hand or electric
A rotary whisk or a hand-held mixer	useful if you have only a heavy electric mixer

Very important when planning work surfaces is to allow for more electric socket outlets than you think you will ever need. Your collection of small electric appliances is bound to grow as you acquire the kettle, coffee percolator, toaster, coffee grinder, not to mention mixer and blender, that turn the chore of food preparation into a pleasure.

Pressure cooker

A valuable piece of equipment for the thrifty-minded housewife. It not only cooks and tenderises cheaper cuts of meat quickly (it cuts down the time needed for a casserole by two-thirds) but it cooks without waste, makes stock for soup, cooks root vegetables and steamed puddings, *and* it saves fuel. A lot of people have told me that they're a little scared of the pressure cooker. Don't be. I have used mine happily and confidently for years. Follow the manufacturer's instructions and you'll find it a valuable money-saver.

Mixer

Here there is a huge range of time-saving and labour-saving devices for the cook. There is the sophisticated electric mixer, with a whole battery of attachments for dealing with the less exciting food-preparation chores — peeling, shredding, liquidising, grinding, juicing, mincing, beating, mixing. There are smaller models with stand and bowl, which will do most of the common mixing tasks; and there are the hand-held models, either small, single-speed whisks, or larger ones with three speeds and perhaps a choice of beaters. I find my hand mixer invaluable; it's always available when I want it and there is no elaborate setting-up of bowls and attachments involved.

Blender

Then there are the blenders or liquidisers. They have a value to the money-saving cook out of all proportion to their cost, which in fact is comparatively low. They deal with liquids or with very soft foods that have a high liquid content — soups, purées, baby foods — which the ordinary mixing bowl could not accommodate. They can also be used for making breadcrumbs, grating cheese, and rubbing fat into flour.

Yogurt-maker

If you really like yogurt, it's worth investing in a maker. But see my method for making yogurt in an airing cupboard (page 80).

Home freezer

The refrigerator and the freezer have between them made the kitchen revolution of this century. They are the biggest kitchen investments you are likely to make and the ones that will give you the biggest return — in economy, in health and safety, in variety, in a whole new world of cooking and catering — whether your family is large or small, whatever your individual needs may be.

The refrigerator has been with us for many years and is now considered an essential in every kitchen. It keeps perishable foods clean and fresh and models with special frozen-food compartments will store foods for up to three months depending on rating. The home freezer has not taken its place. The two complement each other; they're not interchangeable. Used together, they're your biggest single money-saver.

Freezing at temperatures of $-18°C$ ($-0.4°F$) or below is the easiest, most natural and safest way to preserve food. Most foods, if properly packed and frozen, can be kept for long periods (in some cases up to a year) in perfect safety with very little loss of quality or flavour. The frozen-food compartment of the refrigerator can store only for a limited period. The freezer on the other hand both freezes and stores fresh food and stores already frozen food.

With a freezer you have a safe store of perishables to be called upon at any time — particularly in emergencies when you're faced with unexpected mouths to feed. You can freeze the produce of your own garden at its freshest and best; you can buy fruit and vegetables in season, when they're at their cheapest, to use later when prices in the shops have rocketed; you can have a constant supply of bread and cakes. Furthermore you can cook in quantity when you feel like it and when you have the opportunity — it could be when the children are at school, at weekends, or when the weather is bad and you're not tempted to go out. Making twice the quantity you need, you can eat half now and freeze the rest to eat later.

There is another bonus. With a freezer you can prepare basic supplies in bulk. Make a big quantity of stock from chicken carcasses or meat bones and store it to use as you want for soups, sauces and gravies. Prepare a quantity of basic white or brown sauce and store; you can add flavourings as required later. Do the same with minced beef, the basis of many savoury dishes — meat loaf, meatballs, fillings for pies, bolognese sauce for spaghetti, etc. And the same principle applies to bread and cake mixtures — prepare the basic mixture in bulk and then ring the changes with the finished product. You can in fact enjoy a new freedom, secure in the knowledge that the food supply is assured.

Freezers are made in three basic types: the chest type, the upright, and the refrigerator-freezer, which has two separate doors and combines an upright freezer with a refrigerator in one cabinet, very useful where space in the kitchen is at a premium. Buy the type that suits you best, bearing in mind where it is to be kept and the space at your disposal. And buy the best and biggest you can afford. It is only when you have used a freezer for a while that you will realise what it can do for you — and that may be the time when you wish you had bought a bigger one.

What *can* it do for you, particularly in regard to what we're all interested in — simply saving money?

First of all, waste is virtually eliminated. Frightening statistics are published from time to time concerning the amount of food thrown into the dustbins of this country. Thoughtlessly we buy food that we don't need — to be on the safe side. The food is not used; it goes bad and is thrown away. Think of the money that is thrown away with it. With a freezer in the kitchen this does not happen. Anything left over can be safely stored ready to be used when needed.

Furthermore the freezer has brought about a revolution in buying habits. Where the housewife used to make a twice-weekly or even daily visit to the shops to buy food for immediate use,

paying full retail prices for small quantities, she now shops at extended intervals. There are various ways of doing this. You can place a bulk order with a freezer supply centre once a month or once a quarter, visit a supermarket and come away with half a dozen frozen chickens or a jumbo-size pack of vegetables at an advantageous price; or you can order half a carcass from a specialist butcher who will cut it into convenient joints for storage in the freezer. All this will be done at a considerable saving — reduced prices for quantity.

One side of freezer ownership that gives a lot of pleasure is growing your own fruit and vegetables for freezing. Not only do you save money on shop prices, you pick your produce when it's at its best. Even the smallest garden has room for a few rows of beans, peas, cauliflower, onions; and many people with gardens have an apple tree or two that will produce a glut of fruit in the autumn. If you live in the country, most of your neighbours are experiencing the same thing and nobody can give away their fruit. The freezer comes to the rescue. Grow your own strawberries, raspberries, red and black currants and enjoy them out of season as well as in summer. Experiment with interesting vegetables like asparagus and corn on the cob, which freeze well.

If you have no garden and your gardening friends can't keep you supplied, try market or roadside stalls; they often have supplies in season at a reasonable price. Better still, go to one of the farms or market gardens that will allow you, now that labour is hard to come by, to pick your own fruit and vegetables at an economical price. In this way you're sure of getting the best and the freshest available.

A word about convenience foods. You may well be tempted to keep a stock of these in the freezer, but do remember that the handy, ready-cooked pack that claims to be a 'dinner for two' often turns out to hold barely enough for one and a half reasonable appetites. For the same money you could buy enough ingredients to make a meal for four people.

So the money-saving moral is, buy in bulk, cook in quantity, freeze in convenient portions. Your freezer will then repay the money spent on it.

Chapter 2
Making the most of food

Time, we are told, is money. These practical tips are intended to help you save on both. I've tried all of them. They work.

Shopping

This is where it all begins. Best general advice is, work to a plan. Random shopping can be fun—it can be expensive, too.

Cut down your shopping trips. Once a week may be ideal; twice if you must. Freezer owners will soon discover the advantages of one big bulk-buying expedition over a series of short trips to the shops.

Keep a shopping list to which you add items as they run low—saves emergency dashes for a packet of salt or a pound of rice.

Shop around. Look out for bargains and cheap offers in supermarkets. But do it within a reasonable radius of your home; there's no saving if you lose on petrol or travelling time what you save in the shop.

Buy frozen or refrigerated goods in the supermarket rather than in the corner shop. Supermarkets have a quick turnover and food there is likely to be fresher.

If possible, shop when you have plenty of time. Early in the week is good, as fresh produce tends to become more expensive towards the weekend—although late on Saturday afternoons you can often pick up bargains in markets where goods are being sold off.

Buy the exact amount that you require of perishable goods you don't often use, unless you can spare the room to store them in the freezer; it's no economy to buy a pack of four green peppers when you can buy the one that the recipe demands.

Read labels carefully and be sure that you know just what you're paying for.

When you are trying something for the first time, buy the smallest quantity available; you may not like it.

When canned goods or other staple foods are on special offer, stock up your store cupboard. But check to see if similar items on the shelves are not cheaper.

When larger amounts than you need or can conveniently store are on offer at a good discount, get together with friends and divide a big quantity among yourselves.

Use special reduction coupons only if you would buy the product anyway, or at least only if you would be willing to try it at the full price.

To keep frozen foods, meat and fish at their best, buy them after you've done the rest of the shopping. Pack them together in one bag to keep cold and don't leave them in the car while you attend to something else.

Meat, poultry and fish

These are the sources of protein most of us prefer, but it is a fact that most of us prefer more of these proteins than we need. The most active teenager, who should have as much as, if not more than, his father, requires only the equivalent of 4 ounces (100 grams) of cooked meat a day, plus milk and other protein foods. Cheese contains as much protein as meat and costs less.

Here are some equivalents of 1 ounce (25 grams) of meat:

$\frac{1}{2}$ pint (250 millilitres) milk
2 ounces (50 grams) cottage cheese
4 ounces (100 grams) cooked broad beans
1 ounce (25 grams) peanut butter

Consider servings per pound or kilogram when you compare costs:

Boneless lean meat, fish and poultry give 3–4 servings.
Chops, fish steaks (with bone) and chicken portions give 2–3 servings.

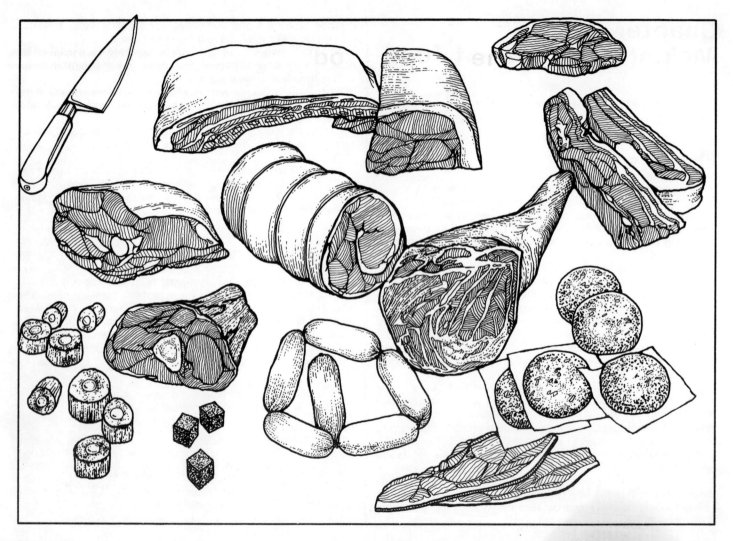

Fatty or bony meats (spare ribs, whole fish, chicken wings) give 1–2 servings.

Take advantage of reduced prices for bulk orders of cheaper cuts of meat and poultry. Cook and then freeze in family-size portions.

Save and freeze poultry livers until you have enough to make pâté.

Study the different cuts of meat and compare prices.

Bacon

When buying bacon, try forehock, gammon slipper, and collar. Use streaky bacon in place of back.

Buy bacon pieces to chop up for flans and pies.

Save bacon rinds; fry them (or crisp when you're using the oven) and serve to nibble with drinks. Use rinds for flavouring soups and casseroles too. (Easiest way to remove rind is with kitchen scissors.)

Save bacon fat for frying vegetables for soups and stews.

Beef

Brisket and topside of beef are cheaper than sirloin; stewing steak is always cheaper than rump. Other cheap cuts: chuck steak, shoulder steak, skirt, mince, shin.

From these cheaper cuts you can make stews, casseroles, rag-outs of all kinds, pies and pasties, soups and sauces.

Chicken

A good buy for the family. Freezer owners will know the advantage of buying several chickens at a time when they're going cheaply. Choose a whole chicken rather than pieces – it will provide several meals.

Bones and giblets	make stock for soup.
Liver	use for pâté or as flavouring for risotto.

Lamb

Shoulder, neck and breast of lamb are economy cuts that cook deliciously.

Cheap cuts make hotpot, stew, Scotch broth; breast of lamb can be stuffed, rolled and baked in the oven.

Pork

Hand and belly of pork can be used in casseroles, though you may find it a little fatty; it's better for grilling or roasting where the excess fat may be drained off. Spare-rib chops, which go well with sweet and sour sauce, can be substituted for loin chops.

Turkey

Today's specialised breeding methods have produced smaller birds with broad, plump breasts and the minimum of waste. A turkey is a boon to freezer owners; it will provide a variety of family meals. Cut up a partially thawed bird and prepare dishes that can be re-frozen after cooking.

Legs and thighs	casserole with vegetables.
Wings	simmer with vegetables for stew.
Breasts	slice thinly and use as chicken or veal cutlets; or cut into strips for quick fried dishes.
Left-overs	cut from carcass and use for pies.
Carcass	make stock for soup.

Making meat go further

No wise cook will serve any kind of meat on its own. Additions are endless; vegetables are obvious. One pound (half kilo) of meat is usually considered enough for four people, but it can stretch to feed six if enough vegetables are used. Don't serve just one vegetable, however, use a variety. As well as bulk, they add flavour to the casserole and give a distinctive taste to the stew.

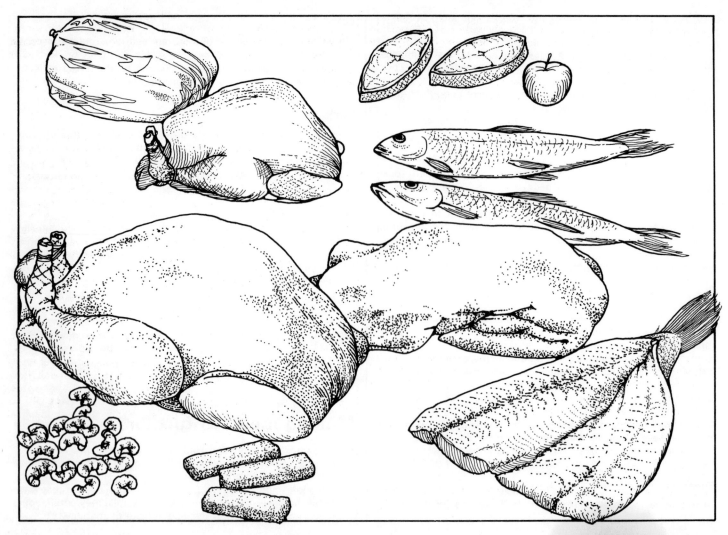

Root vegetables help considerably with bulk and the pressure cooker deals very quickly and satisfactorily with them. Make soup from them too; cook in a good meat or chicken stock and purée in the electric blender—quick and easy.

Serve dumplings on cold days with stews or hotpots.

Rice is a good filling accompaniment to meat dishes, and with savoury additions—left-over meat or chicken, bacon scraps, put through the mincer or blender—it can become a dish on its own.

Fill out meat, poultry or even fish dishes with dried peas, beans, lentils, baked beans; they add bulk and protein very economically.

Pasta of all kinds is economical. It usually needs only the addition of a well-flavoured sauce and grated cheese to sprinkle over it. Served with a green salad from the garden, it's a meal in its own right.

Stuffings, with breadcrumbs (made in the blender from left-over bread and stored in the freezer), herbs and flavourings added, give bulk and can turn cheap cuts of lamb into a feast—and they work miracles for the rather bland taste of frozen chickens.

Vegetable 'meat'

A money-saver of the future? A substitute for meat, produced mainly from soya beans (which incidentally yield thirty times as much protein per acre as beef cattle) is already on the market and is gaining ground. Vegetarians and health-food addicts have been using vegetable protein in place of meat in their diet for some time, but it's only lately that there has been wide-scale research into producing a really acceptable meat substitute. It's a development worth watching, certainly from the money-saving angle.

Left-over cooked meat

Don't throw it away. Purée it in the liquidiser and add stock to make soup.

Or use it as a filling for pies and pasties.

Or carve remaining meat from cooked joint and layer in a casserole with sliced carrots and onions, add stock and seasoning. Top with suet crust and bake in moderate oven for about an hour.

Fish

The price of fresh fish varies with the season and especially with the weather—a few storms and the price rockets to well above the level of frozen fish; after good catches the price will drop and fish will become a much better buy. Frozen fish is often prepared frozen at sea so should be in a good condition when it reaches the shops. Fresh fish can vary considerably—look for shops with a good standard of hygiene and a quick turnover.

Buy large fish fingers, not smaller ones (the bread coating accounts for about 50 per cent of the total). But fish can very quickly be dipped in home-made batter to give you better value for money. If only a little fish is being dipped, set some batter on one side for apple fritters the following day, or dilute with milk and make into pancakes.

When buying fresh fish look for a firm flesh, bright not sunken eyes and with scales not flaking off. Crabs, lobsters and fish in their shells should feel heavy for their size, indicating well-filled shells; mussels should close quickly when tapped.

Make cod steaks, coley and other white fish more interesting with a good sauce. For example, try a white sauce with fried chopped mushroom stalks or chopped parsley, a cheese sauce, or paprika and tomato. For a sauce Provençal see page 36. All of these can be poured over raw fish steaks and fillets, then baked to make an easy tasty meal. For more ideas, see page 34.

Sauces

In cooking a sauce—whether a white sauce, brown sauce or gravy—the first stage is to melt the fat (butter or dripping) and add the flour. This combination is called the 'roux' and although a recipe usually calls for equal quantities of fat and flour—one ounce perhaps of each—it is important that the weight of fat should be generous.

The roux should not make a firm ball but should run flat, otherwise you will have a lumpy sauce. If roux looks too dry, add a little more fat. For a white sauce cook the roux for two or three minutes and take off the heat; for a brown sauce or gravy, allow the flour to brown before removing. With the pan away from the heat, add almost half of the cold liquid stirring quickly. When mixture is smooth, add the remainder before returning to the heat and bringing to the boil stirring constantly.

For a white sauce it is possible to put all the ingredients together in the pan without making a roux and whisk while bringing to the boil; but don't ruin non-stick pans by this method.

Herbs and spices

Flavouring is all important to the imaginative cook. It makes all the difference between an ordinary run-of-the-mill dish and one that sets the family asking for more. Keep a good stock of all kinds of herbs—fresh and dried. So much the better if you can grow your own; a few pots on the kitchen window sill can be the basis of a flourishing herb garden and a lot of improved cooking.

Stock your cupboard with a collection of spices and ring the changes with these. Sea salt and black peppercorns, to grind in a pepper mill as required, show that you are a cook who cares.

Vegetables and fruit

They're usually cheaper in season—although their frozen equivalents, having no waste, often work out at about the same price.

Grow your own if you can. Even if you have no garden, you can probably have a few tomato plants on the window sill.

Seasonal fruit chart

△=at peak of season and most likely to be reasonable to buy
□=available in shops

	Jan	Feb	Mar	Apr	May	Jun	Jul	Aug	Sep	Oct	Nov	Dec
Apples cooking	□	□	□	□	□	□	□	□	△	△	△	△
dessert	△	□	□	□	□	□	□	□	△	△	△	△
Apricots	□	□			△	△	△	△				□
Avocado pears					available all year							
Bananas					available all year							
Bilberries							□	△	△			
Blackberries									△	△		
Blackcurrants						□	△	△				
Cherries					□	△	△	△				
Chinese gooseberries									△	△	△	△
Cranberries	△	△										△
Damsons								△	△	△		
Dates (fresh)	□	□	□							□	□	□
Figs									△	△	△	
Gooseberries				△	△	□						
Grapes	□	□	□	□	□	□	△	△	△	△	△	□
Grapefruit	△	△	□	□	□	□	□	□	□	□	△	△
Greengages								△	△			
Lemons	△	△	□	□	□	□	□	□	△	△	△	△
Limes	△	△							△	△	△	△
Lychees	△	△										△
Loganberries							△	△				
Mandarins	△	△	△									△
Mangoes	△	△	△	△	△	△	□					
Medlars											□	□
Melons	□	□	□	□	□	△	△	△	△	△	△	□

Seasonal fruit chart

	Jan	Feb	Mar	Apr	May	Jun	Jul	Aug	Sep	Oct	Nov	Dec
Oranges				available all year								
Passion fruit	□	□	□									
Peaches	□	□				△	△	△	△	□		□
Pears	□	□	□		□	△	△	△	△	△	△	□
Pineapple					available all year							
Plums						△	△	△	△	△	□	□
Pomegranates									△	△	△	
Raspberries						△	△	△	△			
Redcurrants						△	△	△				
Rhubarb	□	□	△	△	□	□	□					
Satsumas	△								△	△	△	△
Seville oranges	△	△	△									△
Strawberries					□	△	△	△				
Tomatoes	□	□	□	□	□	△	△	△	□	□	□	□

Seasonal vegetable chart

△=at peak of season and most likely to be reasonable to buy
□=available in shops

	Jan	Feb	Mar	Apr	May	Jun	Jul	Aug	Sep	Oct	Nov	Dec
Artichokes globe						□	△	△	△	□	□	
Artichokes Jerusalem	△	△	△	△								
Asparagus	△	△	△									
Aubergines	□						△	△	△	△	□	
Beetroot					available all year							
Broad beans					△	△	△					
Broccoli	△	△	△	△	△				△		△	△
Brussels sprouts	△	△	□	□					□	□	△	△
Cabbage					available all year							
Capsicums							□		□			
Carrots	△	△	△	△	△	△	△				△	□
Cauliflower	□	□	□	□	□	□	□		□	□	□	□
Celeriac	△	△	△	□					△	△	△	△
Celery	△	△		□	□				□	□	△	△
Chicory	□	□	□	□	□					□	△	△
Chillis						△	△	△				
Corn on the cob								△	△	△		
Courgettes					□	△	△	△	△	△		
Cucumber	□	□	□	□	△	△	△	△	△	□	□	□
Endive		□	□	□				△	△	△		
Fennel	□								△	△	△	□
French beans						△	△	△	△			
Garlic				available all year								
Kohl rabi						△	△	△	△			
Leeks	△	△	△	□						△	△	△
Lettuce	□	□	□	□	△	△	△	△	△	□	□	□
Mange-tout peas						△	△			△	△	
Marrows								△	△		△	△
Mushrooms cultivated				available all year								
Mushrooms field								△	△	△		
Onions	□	□	□	□	□	□	□	□	△	△	△	△
Parsley				available all year								
Parsnips	△	△	△	□						□	□	△
Peas						△	△	△	△	□		
Potatoes (new)					□	△	△	△	□			
Pumpkin									□	△	□	
Radish	□	□	□	□	△	△	△	△	□	□	□	□
Runner beans							△	△	△			
Seakale	△	△	△									
Spinach	□	□	□	△	△	△	□	□	□	□	□	□
Spring greens			△	△	△	△						
Swedes	△	△	△	□					□	□	△	△
Turnips	□	△	△	□	□				△	△	□	□
Watercress	△	△	△	□	□	□				□	□	□

Frozen or canned vegetables or fruits usually cost less sliced or chopped than whole.

Fruit and vegetables keep better if you don't wash them until just before you use them. If moisture is left on for any length of time, it can cause mould and rot.

Apples

To prevent discolouring, put them in cold salt water when you peel them – 1 tablespoon of salt to 2 pints (1 litre) water – rinse with cold water before cooking.

If you have more apples than you know what to do with, take the easy way out and make apple jelly. No peeling is needed and the jelly will be a good colour. You can add chopped mint to make mint jelly.

Bananas

It's better to buy them under-ripe rather than over-ripe. This is one fruit that ripens in store. On no account put bananas in the refrigerator; they'll turn black.

Beetroot

Before boiling, remove only the top leaves and take care not to pierce the skin or the colour will bleed out of the beetroot.

Dried vegetables

Useful if you need only a small amount – for example, sliced onions or mixed vegetables.

You can buy dried, chopped green and red peppers in small pots. These are economical as you need only a small amount for flavouring casseroles, sauces and stews, or to use in omelettes and salads. Soak them for five minutes in boiling water and they are ready for use.

Frozen vegetables

Buy plain varieties and dress them up as you like – with a special sauce; or an additional flavouring.

Fruit salad

You can make a good one out of fruit bought cheaply – at a local market perhaps. Prepare the fruit and arrange it in a dish in layers with caster sugar – about 2–4 ounces (50–100 grams) sugar per pound ($\frac{1}{2}$ kilo) of fruit. Finish with a layer of sugar and chill overnight so that a fruit syrup is formed.

Jerusalem artichokes

Make an excellent soup and can be served as a vegetable too. Boil until barely tender, then plunge in cold water and peel. If you're using them for soup, return to pan and cook until soft; to serve as a vegetable, finish off cooking in butter.

Leeks

One of the best vegetables of all – must be well cleaned.

Lemons

When squeezing don't take them straight from the refrigerator. Better use a lemon at room temperature and warm it in your hand first – you'll get more juice.

Never waste lemon or orange rind. Grate it finely, add caster sugar and store in separate screw-top jars; use to flavour cakes and puddings.

Mushrooms

There's no need to peel the cultivated kind; just wash and pat dry on kitchen paper.

Oranges

Buy thin-skinned ones for fruit salad.

Parsley and mint

To keep parsley or mint, chop, add water and freeze in the ice-cube tray. When frozen, remove from tray, wrap each cube individually in foil and store in freezer.

Peppers

To keep a partly used fresh green or red pepper, remove the seeds and slice or chop the flesh. Wrap and freeze.

Potatoes

Cook them in their skins—the best part is just under the skin. Peel them or not as you like; eat them with butter.

If you use a lot of potatoes, it's cheaper to buy them by the sack and store in a dry, cool, dark place.

Stewing fruit

Be careful not to overcook or it will lose its shape—apples and rhubarb very easily turn mushy. Cook gently until tender, then remove from heat. Alternatively, cook slowly in the oven when you're cooking a casserole.

Tomatoes

To skin, plunge them in boiling water, then in cold, and the skin will peel off easily.

Trimmings

Don't waste them. Outside leaves, the green parts of leeks, leaves of celery, can be used in soups.

Making vegetables more interesting

Combine two or more vegetables to make them more interesting: a casserole of new potatoes in a white sauce with cooked mushrooms or Jerusalem artichokes; apples and onions in a casserole of drumhead cabbage; cucumber with minted peas, either hot or as a salad.

Make expensive vegetables go further: add boiled onions, peas or tomatoes to courgettes; carrots to broad beans in parsley sauce; a few potatoes to a purée of delicious celeriac.

For special occasions finish a dish of French beans with a topping of almonds fried in butter or braised celery with toasted walnuts. Try cauliflower finished with fried wholemeal breadcrumbs instead of a sauce for a change; try beetroot hot with a dash of vinegar, a sprinkle of sugar and dill.

Use all those oddments up in the vegetable rack—carrots, onions, celery, parsnips, swedes, potatoes—cut up into matchsticks and cooked very slowly in a casserole, or cooked in just a little butter and served sprinkled with chopped herbs.

A combination of carrot, onion and celery is inexpensive, tasty and attractive enough to serve when entertaining.

Dairy produce

Eggs

These are now sold in date-stamped boxes. Buy fresh and store in the refrigerator if you're keeping them for more than ten days. Store them pointed end down. This is not a superstition; there's an air pocket at the top that prevents the yolk from rising during storage and sticking to the shell.

Look out for fresh eggs on offer in the country. If you're lucky, you may be able to buy fresh, cracked eggs at a very much reduced price. These are ideal for scrambled eggs, omelettes, baking. Use within a week of purchase.

You will get best results when making cakes or meringues by using eggs at room temperature.

When a recipe needs either the white or the yolk of an egg, don't waste the other half.

Left-over yolks: cover with water in a cup or small bowl and store in the refrigerator. Use to enrich sauces and soups.

Left-over whites: store just as they are in a covered container. Use to make meringue; or add to scrambled eggs or omelettes.

Cheese

Save those odd-shaped pieces for cooking; grate when dry and keep in rigid plastic containers in the refrigerator.

Mild Cheddar is usually cheaper than mature Cheddar as it has a shorter ripening life.

It's cheaper to buy grated Parmesan cheese in plastic, 500-gram screw-top jars than in 1-ounce drums. Cheese specialists and good delicatessens sell it and it will keep in the refrigerator for six months; in the freezer for a year or more.

Milk and cream

Condensed milk: not cheap but it does add richness and is excellent in recipes like the lemon flan on page 75.

Double cream: it's more economical to buy it in a large carton for recipes asking for a large amount. On the other hand, you can use equal quantities of single and double cream; just whip the two together.

Dried low-fat milk: made from skimmed milk, it's cheaper than fresh and keeps well. Can be added to batters, soups and sauces. Good for slimmers. Can be given double strength to children or invalids.

Evaporated milk: you can make a cheap mock cream by chilling evaporated milk. In a chilled bowl whip a small can of evaporated milk with a rotary whisk or a mixer, add a level tablespoon of caster sugar and a few drops of vanilla essence. You'll find that the original amount of milk has trebled. Good for pouring on fruit, pies and puddings of different kinds.

Evaporated milk is cheaper than fresh milk for sauces, flan fillings and puddings; it makes a very creamy rice pudding, and for mousses it can be chilled and whisked with the addition of a fruit, coffee or chocolate flavouring.

Long-life single cream: will keep for two to three months out of the refrigerator.

Soured cream: costs a little more than the single cream from which it is made. It will keep up to seven days in a refrigerator. Much used in northern and central European cooking; it can be added to goulash, mayonnaise, cheesecake, salad dressings.

Bread

Enriched white bread is less expensive per pound than whole-meal.

Don't waste bread. Freeze it and it will keep for up to three months.

Cut stale loaves into thin slices, remove crusts and bake bread in a slow oven (300°F, 150°C, gas mark 2) until golden, to make melba toast for serving with soups and pâtés.

Spread slices of slightly stale bread with butter or margarine and sprinkle lightly with one of these: garlic salt, onion salt, curry powder. Wrap bread in foil and heat in moderate oven (350°F, 175°C, gas mark 4) for half an hour.

Biscuits

Buy loose when you can. Most have been rejected by the manufacturer for some small defect in shape or size; but they're just as good as, and cheaper than, the packaged variety.
Buy plain water biscuits to go with cheese.

Brown breadcrumbs

Make your own by cooking crusts in a slow oven until quite dry. Then either crush with a rolling pin or mince finely. Store in freezer.

Cereals

Buy in large boxes rather than individual packets.

Muesli

Make your own from oats, dried fruit, nuts. Store in an airtight jar.

Puddings and sweets

Serve good filling ones in cold weather: dumplings filled with your own apples from store, steamed suet puddings (the pressure cooker again), fruit tarts and pies. And all the fruits of summer can go into the blender to emerge as fools and purées at the touch of a switch. For gala dishes, whipped cream is increased in bulk by beating in the white of an egg.

Does it look good?

Presentation of a dish is half the battle, so make your cooking as attractive as you can. From the croûtons in the soup to the cherry on top of the trifle, it is the details that count. So remember the importance of garnishes, a really inexpensive means of giving a dish the professional touch, bringing it up to party standards.

Fresh parsley—you can grow your own in that pot on the window sill—is a simple and effective bit of colour. Judicious slices of tomato—when cheap—or of lemon or sweet peppers, can work wonders. You have faith in your cooking. You know the dish tastes good; make it look good too.

Miscellaneous economies

A filling but less expensive first course such as soup or a good salad takes the edge off appetites, so that smaller servings of the more expensive main course will be needed.

Make your own soups—much cheaper than buying them in cans or packets.

Make your own salad dressing and mayonnaise. Make large quantities at a time and store.

Buy large cans of cooking oil rather than small bottles. Fry in a small amount of oil. When you deep fry, strain the oil and keep it in a refrigerator to use again.

Keep wrappers from fat, butter, margarine. Store in a plastic bag and use to grease baking tins.

Make your own jam and marmalade from fruits in season.

In recipes calling for the addition of wine, cider can often be used instead.

Instead of buying expensive containers for use in the freezer, line a dish with foil, add the food (cooked or uncooked) and freeze. Remove from dish when frozen and wrap in more foil. Store. When wanted, put back in the original dish for re-heating or cooking.

Plastic yogurt tubs make good containers for use in the freezer.

If you're cooking a casserole in the oven—and the cooking has to be long and slow—try to put in several dishes at once so that the best use is made of fuel.

The last drop . . .

Get the last out of a tube of tomato purée, or mustard, or toothpaste. Screw the cap on tightly. Put the tube on the kitchen floor and stand on the end farther from the cap. Flatten the tube, pushing the remaining contents towards the cap. Roll up the flattened tube and you'll have an extra drop or two for your efforts.

Chapter 3
Starters

The start of a meal should set the mood and get everyone into the right frame of mind for what is to follow. It should also complement the rest of the menu. If the main course is filling or rich, the starter must be light and delicate, sufficient to whet the appetite rather than deaden it. Equally, a frothy main course needs a more satisfying starter.

Of course some starters, such as soups, can be so good that they're almost a meal in themselves. And when served for supper or as snacks, that's just what they are. For nutritional value and flavour, there is little to beat a home-made soup and it ranks high on the popularity charts of most families.

What's best about soup from the housewife's point of view is that it's a wonderful way of using up little bits of left-overs. Cooked meat and vegetables can be liquidised and blended with stock to make soup that is satisfying as well as tasty. A bouillon cube can be used if you have no home-made stock available.

Most in-season vegetables make excellent soup. If you grow your own, and have no freezer in which to store the surplus, use what you can't eat in the normal way to make soup. With a little care, your family won't even realise there's been a glut and, what's more, it won't have cost you one penny extra.

Onion soup is cheap and simple to make, while home-made tomato soup can be steaming in bowls on the table just ten minutes after you start to prepare it.

Then there are special-occasion and unusual soups. Green pepper soup, for example, will be much appreciated by those who have acquired a taste for this strongly flavoured vegetable. Again, if your garden has yielded a mountain of lettuces and straight salads have begun to pall, use some of them to make a lettuce soup, which is blander in flavour than the other two. Or try the yogurt and tomato soup, which is excellent in summer as it is served cold and needs no cooking.

Starters need not be confined to soups. Old favourites like egg mayonnaise or grapefruit benefit from some variation, which can be provided easily at little extra cost. And pâtés, made from inexpensive ingredients, are always good for kicking off a meal when you have guests.

French onion soup

If making this soup for Sunday night supper, use stock made from the joint bones if you had beef, or from the carcass of chicken. If you have good beef dripping in the fridge, also add the rich jelly that settles underneath the dripping. It adds to the flavour.

Preparation time: 15 minutes
Cooking time: 30–40 minutes
Serves 4

2 oz (50 g) lard or dripping
1 lb (500 g) onions
1 oz (25 g) flour
1½ pt (750 ml) stock or
1½ pt (750 ml) water and 2 chicken stock cubes
2 tsp tomato purée
Salt and pepper
4 slices French bread
3 heaped tbsp Cheddar cheese

Heat the dripping in a pan. Peel and finely chop the onions and add to the pan; fry until beginning to brown. Blend in flour and cook gently to brown, then add the stock, tomato purée and seasonings. Bring to boiling point, stirring, and simmer covered for 30–40 minutes. Check seasoning.

Toast bread under grill, then put cheese on and brown. Float in soup the moment before it is served.

To prepare in advance: Soup can be made up to 24 hours ahead.

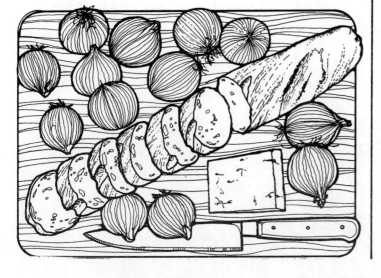

Quick tomato soup

A home-made soup that takes just 15 minutes to make. If you have fresh basil in the garden, sprinkle a little chopped on top of each bowlful when serving.

Preparation time: 5 minutes
Cooking time: 10 minutes
Serves 4

1 small onion
1 oz (25 g) butter or margarine
1 oz (25 g) flour
½ pt (250 ml) milk
½ pt (250 ml) water
4 tbsp tomato purée
1 level tsp caster sugar
Salt and pepper
Pinch mixed dried herbs
Chopped parsley

Peel and finely chop the onion. Melt the butter in a pan and fry the onion without colouring until soft. Stir in the flour and cook for 1–2 minutes without browning. Draw the pan to one side of the heat. Gradually add the milk and water, stirring until smooth, then add the tomato purée. Stir in the sugar, seasoning and herbs. Simmer gently for 7 minutes or until the onion is cooked. Adjust seasoning if necessary. Serve sprinkled with parsley.

Smooth green pepper soup

Frozen peppers are sometimes cheaper than fresh ones so use them for this soup. And if you have stuffed peppers and don't need the tops freeze them (if you have a freezer) and use them for this soup. A blender is not used for puréeing this soup as the fine pieces of pepper skins will still remain; they are completely removed only by sieving. Pepper soup is a soup for entertaining as it tastes most unusual and is delicious.

Preparation time: 20 minutes
Cooking time: 35 minutes
Serves 4

2 tbsp oil
2 oz (50 g) butter or margarine
$\frac{1}{2}$ lb (225 g) green peppers, seeded and diced
2 onions, chopped
1$\frac{1}{2}$ oz (40 g) flour
$\frac{3}{4}$ pt (375 ml) water
2 chicken stock cubes
Salt and pepper
$\frac{3}{4}$ pt (375 ml) milk
2–3 tbsp single cream or top of the milk.

Heat oil in a pan, add fat, then vegetables and cook gently for 5 minutes. Blend in flour and cook 1 minute. Add water and stock cubes, bring to boiling point, add seasoning, then cover and simmer for 30 minutes or until vegetables are soft. Reduce to a purée by sieving, then return to pan with milk. Heat through gently and check seasoning. Add cream or top of the milk just before serving. Serve either hot or very cold with extra cream.

To prepare in advance: Purée the soup but don't add the milk. Put the purée in the refrigerator for up to 24 hours ahead. Just before serving, reheat purée and add milk and top of milk.

Cream of lettuce soup

A very good way of using up a glut of lettuces. In the summer serve the soup chilled. Best made and eaten on the same day.

Preparation time: 15 minutes
Cooking time: 20 minutes
Serves 4

3 oz (75 g) butter or margarine
Small bunch chives
1 large lettuce (a bolted one is ideal), shredded
1 onion, roughly chopped
1 potato, peeled and roughly chopped
1 oz (25 g) flour
$\frac{3}{4}$ pt (375 ml) water
1 chicken stock cube
$\frac{3}{4}$ pt (375 ml) milk
$\frac{1}{4}$ tsp ground nutmeg
Salt and black pepper
Top of the milk

Melt fat, add chives and vegetables. Cover and cook over low heat for 10 minutes. Sprinkle in flour and stir well over heat; add water, stirring well until thickened. Add crumbled cube, milk and seasonings. Simmer for 10 minutes or until the vegetables are soft. Strain off liquid and sieve or purée vegetables in a blender. Return both to pan. Reheat until piping hot. Check seasoning and add the top of the milk to each bowl.

Summer tomato soup

A quick-to-make soup that doesn't need cooking. Use your own home-made yogurt if you prefer. It's very much a sophisticated taste (I found it unpopular with my younger children).

Preparation time: 5 minutes
Serves 6

1 pt (500 ml) natural yogurt
1 pt (500 ml) tomato juice
Juice and grated rind of 1 lemon
$\frac{1}{2}$ cucumber, peeled and cut into $\frac{1}{4}$ in (0·5 cm) cubes
Salt
Freshly ground black pepper
Worcester sauce to taste
Cucumber slices for garnish

Whisk together yogurt and tomato juice. Stir in lemon juice, grated lemon rind and cucumber. Season well and add Worcester sauce. Serve chilled and garnished with thin slices of cucumber.

To prepare in advance: Make up to 24 hours in advance and chill in refrigerator

Carrot soup

For a special occasion add a spoonful of cream and a sprinkle of chives to each soup bowl. Carrot soup is delicious served chilled, but replace butter with oil for this.

Preparation time: 10 minutes
Cooking time: 25 minutes
Serves 4

1 lb (500 g) carrots
1 small onion
1 oz (25 g) butter
1¼ pt (625 ml) water
1 chicken stock cube
2 pieces orange peel
1 bay leaf
Salt and pepper

Peel and slice carrots and onions and cook gently in butter in a covered pan for 5 minutes. Pour on the water, crumble in the stock cube and add the pieces of orange peel (peel from an orange with a potato peeler). Add the bay leaf and seasoning and bring to the boil; simmer for 15 minutes. Cool slightly, remove bay leaf and then sieve or liquidise. Reheat, adjusting seasoning, and serve.

To prepare in advance: Make up to 24 hours in advance.
To freeze: Carrot soup freezes well.

Mushroom soup

A very good mushroom soup that can be made more cheaply by using mushroom stalks for extra flavour when these are obtainable.

Preparation time: 15 minutes
Cooking time: 20 minutes
Serves 4

4 oz (100 g) flat mushrooms
4 oz (100 g) mushroom stalks
1 onion
2 oz (50 g) butter
1 oz (25 g) flour
1½ pt (750 ml) water
1 chicken stock cube
Salt and pepper
1 tsp mint, chopped

Wash mushrooms and cut off the stalks. Chop both finely. Thinly slice the onion and cook gently in a covered pan with the butter and chopped mushrooms for 5 minutes; stir in the flour. Draw off the heat and stir in water, crumbled stock cube, salt and pepper. Bring to the boil and simmer for 10 minutes. Sprinkle with chopped mint before serving.

To prepare in advance: May be prepared 48 hours in advance but the flavour will change if frozen.

Sprout soup

The perfect way of using up the outer leaves trimmed off sprouts – or those poor-quality sprouts that are no longer firm and compact.

Preparation time: 20 minutes
Cooking time: 30 minutes
Serves 4

8 oz (225 g) sprouts and trimmings
1 medium onion
1 oz (25 g) butter
¾ pt (375 ml) water
1 chicken stock cube
2 tbsp flour
½ pt (250 ml) milk
Pinch grated nutmeg
Salt and black pepper

Wash and roughly chop sprouts and trimmings. Peel and slice the onion, cook slowly in a covered pan with the butter for five minutes. Add the water, crumble in the stock cube and bring to the boil. Add the sprouts to the pan and simmer uncovered for fifteen minutes or until quite tender. Cool slightly, then sieve or liquidise the soup. Blend flour with a little of the milk then add the remainder, stir this into the soup and reheat. Boil for one minute to thicken and season with nutmeg, salt and pepper.

To prepare in advance: Make and purée soup up to 24 hours in advance, but add milk and thicken when reheating to serve.
To freeze: Freeze before adding the milk to ensure the soup has a creamy texture; complete preparation just before serving.

Oeufs aurore

Make this classic egg dish when time is short. It's very good. For a main meal double the quantities in the recipe.

Preparation time: 15 minutes
Cooking time: 10 minutes
Serves 6

½ cucumber, thinly sliced
1 bunch watercress
6 hard-boiled eggs, halved lengthways
8 oz (225 g) home-made or good bought mayonnaise
1 tbsp tomato purée
2 tbsp tomato ketchup
Drop Tabasco sauce
Salt and pepper

Arrange cucumber and watercress on large, flat serving dish, reserving a few sprigs of watercress. Place halved eggs round edge of dish, cut sides downwards. Blend together mayonnaise, tomato purée, tomato ketchup and Tabasco. Check seasoning. Coat eggs with mayonnaise mixture, arranging remaining watercress in centre of dish. Serve with brown bread and butter or margarine.

To prepare in advance: Make mayonnaise, if preferred to shop-bought, and add flavouring. Hard boil eggs. Do this up to 24 hours ahead, then assemble just before the meal.

Eggs with Caesar salad

A variation on the hard-boiled egg theme. The crisp croûtons add an interesting crunch. For a main meal double the quantities in this recipe.

Preparation time: 15 minutes
Cooking time: 10 minutes for eggs
Serves 4

1 large slice bread, decrusted
3 tbsp salad oil
3 tbsp French dressing
1 egg, beaten
2 oz (50 g) can anchovy fillets, chopped
2 oz (50 g) well-flavoured Cheddar cheese, grated
1 Cos lettuce
4 hard-boiled eggs

Cut bread in $\frac{1}{4}$ in (0·5 cm) cubes. Fry in oil until golden brown, drain on kitchen paper, then cover and store. Blend together French dressing, beaten egg, and anchovy fillets. Wash lettuce and store in refrigerator in plastic bag.

Blend dressing mixture with lettuce and cheese. Just before serving, add croûtons and arrange on four individual plates. Halve hard-boiled eggs and arrange two halves on each plate.

To prepare in advance: Prepare croûtons, French dressing and hard-boiled eggs up to 24 hours ahead. Assemble just before the meal.

Shrimp and apple salad

Good starter for slimmers. The expensive shrimps are bulked out with the apples and celery, providing a crunchy change. For a main meal double up the ingredients.

Preparation time: 15 minutes
Serves 6

3 dessert apples, cored and chopped
Juice of $\frac{1}{2}$ lemon
8 sticks celery, chopped
$\frac{1}{4}$ pt (125 ml) good mayonnaise or low-calorie salad cream
4 oz (100 g) shelled shrimps or prawns
2 tsp tomato purée
1 lettuce, washed
6 lemon slices

Mix together all ingredients except lettuce and lemon slices. Place crisp lettuce leaves on six individual plates. Pile shrimp or prawn mixture in centre of plates. Top each with a lemon slice.

To prepare in advance: Best made only a few hours ahead and kept covered in the refrigerator.

Chilled grapefruit with grapes

Make this in the summer when grapes are cheap and plentiful.

Preparation time: 25 minutes
Serves 6

3 large grapefruit
½ lb (225 g) firm white grapes
2 oz (50 g) Demerara sugar

Halve grapefruit, carefully remove segments and put in a bowl. Skin grapes — this is what takes the time — halve and remove seeds. Add to grapefruit segments and mix well. Pile fruit back in grapefruit skins and spoon sugar round edge of each. Chill for several hours before serving.

To prepare in advance: Make up to 24 hours ahead. Cover each grapefruit with plastic wrap and put in refrigerator.
To freeze: Freeze the filling, then serve in glasses when thawed.

Hot ginger grapefruit

At Christmas time stem ginger is a favourite present to give and I am often left with the remains of the jar on the shelf not knowing quite what to do with it. It's good done this way with grapefruit or added to a fresh fruit salad.

Preparation time: 5 minutes
Cooking time: 5 minutes
Serves 4

2 grapefruit
Preserved ginger in syrup
4 level tsp soft brown sugar

Cut grapefruit in half. Divide into segments and remove pips and as much membrane as possible. Pour 1 tbsp of ginger syrup over each grapefruit half. Sprinkle with sugar and arrange slices of ginger round edges. Fill centre cavity with small pieces of ginger. Brown under grill.

To prepare in advance: Cut grapefruit into segments up to 12 hours ahead. Chill.

Swedish pickled herring with cucumber

Buy pickled herrings in cans or jars (ask for lunch herrings or sweet pickled herrings). They are sold in Danish centres, delicatessens and larger supermarkets, and are prepared in a milder cure than rollmops and so are not so sharp.

Preparation time: 10 minutes
Serves 4

$\frac{1}{2}$ cucumber
Salt
4 pickled herrings
2 tbsp good mayonnaise
1 level tsp caster sugar
1 tbsp cider vinegar
1 tsp French mustard
Pepper
5 oz (125 g) soured cream
Watercress sprigs or few slices of cucumber for garnish

Peel cucumber, cut into 1 in (2·5 cm) pencil strips. Put on plate and sprinkle with salt. Drain herrings of vinegar and onion. Cut into bite-sized pieces and arrange on a small, shallow serving dish. Mix mayonnaise, sugar, vinegar and seasonings together. Blend with sour cream. Just before serving, pour off liquid from cucumber and then add cucumber to soured cream sauce. Pour over herrings. Decorate with sprigs of watercress or slices of cucumber. Serve with brown bread and butter.

To prepare in advance: Make sauce. Pour over fish just before serving.

Cauliflower au gratin

Small hot dishes such as cauliflower au gratin go well before a cold and light main dish in summer such as herbed Scotch eggs and salad (page 63).

Preparation time: 15 minutes
Cooking time: 10 minutes
Serves 6

2 lb (1 kg) cauliflower
1½ oz (40 g) butter or margarine
1½ oz (40 g) flour
¾ pt (375 ml) milk
3 oz (75 g) Cheddar cheese, grated
Salt and pepper
½ level tsp made mustard
1 level tbsp Parmesan cheese, grated
2 level tbsp dried breadcrumbs

Break cauliflower into florets and cook in boiling salted water until barely tender. Drain, reserving 4 tbsp cooking liquor. Make a roux (see page 14) with fat and flour, blend in milk and bring to the boil. Simmer 2 minutes and remove from heat. Add Cheddar cheese, seasoning and mustard and stir well until cheese has melted. Add cauliflower and reserved liquor, mixing well. Divide cauliflower among six individual dishes. Mix together Parmesan cheese and breadcrumbs and scatter on top. Reheat under medium grill for 5 minutes.

To prepare in advance: Make completely but do not grill. Cover each with plastic wrap. To reheat, remove wrapping, brown in a hot oven for 15 minutes.
To freeze: Freeze before browning and brown as above when thawed.

Simple kipper pâté

This is a soft creamy pâté made from boil-in-the-bag kippers which speeds up the operation. Serve with lots of hot toast or crisp French bread.

Preparation time: 5 minutes
Cooking time: 15 minutes
Serves 6

6 oz (150 g) packet frozen and buttered kipper fillets
2 tsp lemon juice
2½ oz (65 g) single cream
2½ oz (65 g) double cream, whipped
Salt and pepper

Cook kipper fillets in bag according to instructions on packet. Open bag, reserve juices and peel off kipper skins. Purée kippers in a blender with juices, or mash with a fork until smooth. When paste is cold, stir in lemon juice and single cream. Mix until smooth. Fold in double cream. Check seasoning.

To prepare in advance: Make the pâté and put into covered ramekin dishes. It will keep in the refrigerator for up to 48 hours. Remove from refrigerator 1 hour before serving.
To freeze: Kipper pâté freezes well and is best made in one container rather than six.

Buckling pâté

Smoked buckling are herrings smoked for a long time at a moderately high temperature. The smoking process is very similar to the one used for smoking trout, so buckling doesn't need cooking. Serve as you would smoked trout, with horseradish cream or made into this creamy, piquant pâté. Make in the electric blender if you prefer (it will mix smoother if butter is melted first), then chill till set before serving. It's quite a good idea to buy more buckling than you need for one occasion, as not all fish shops sell it.

Preparation time: 15 minutes
Serves 6

2 large bucklings
4 oz (100 g) softened butter or margarine
2 tbsp lemon juice
2 crushed cloves of garlic
Freshly ground pepper

Drop the buckling into boiling water for a minute, then skin and bone. Pound flesh with a wooden spoon and blend together with softened fat. Add crushed garlic and lemon juice. Season to taste with pepper. Serve with hot toast.

To prepare in advance: Make up to a week ahead and keep covered in the refrigerator until an hour before serving.
To freeze: Buckling pâté freezes extremely well. You can also freeze the whole buckling.

Chapter 4
Meat and fish

Some people come to life only when they're planning a dinner party. Then they will go to endless trouble dressing up the meal, preparing little garnishes and choosing side dishes. Yet the family should be just as deserving of special treatment.

The trouble, I suppose, is that the family's meals have to be prepared every day, whereas guests are fed only occasionally. Yet a little bit of extra care can be repaid over and over again by using cheaper, though no less nourishing, ingredients.

Take fish, for example. In my experience, most children like fish, particularly if it's served with a sauce. Adults, however, tend to prefer more expensive fish—or at least they think they do. But a clever cook can perform some quite magical transformations in her kitchen, treating cod cutlets as halibut, for instance.

As with meat, don't be afraid to try the cheaper kinds of fish. Coley and bream are delicious in a fish pie—and half the price of cod or haddock. Steer clear of expensive fish like fresh salmon, skate, halibut or Dover sole—it's almost always possible to find a substitute, particularly if you take the advice of the fishmonger, who can usually suggest ways of cooking and serving fish you're not familiar with.

If you can't get fresh fish of any sort, buy frozen fish. Commercially frozen within hours of being caught, it's a far better buy than so-called fresh fish that may have sat a long time on the fishmonger's slab.

Where the flavour of the fish is likely to be fairly bland, improve it by adding onions, tomatoes or cheese. Add the luxury touch to common-or-garden fish fingers by serving them with a special sauce—made with capers or delicately flavoured with herbs. Fruit-based sauces go well with mackerel or herrings. And remember too that fish dishes are popular with slimmers and those who while not exactly on a diet do like to watch their figures.

Meat is the biggest buy in most families. It's nourishing, filling, lends itself to a great variety of dishes, and most people like it. It's also expensive.

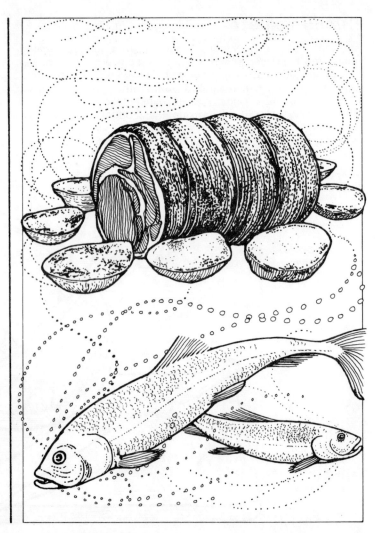

The secret of successful saving here is careful buying and careful preparation and ingenuity. Ignore the groans of the family when they are faced with a dish they've never tried before. You're the one who has to make the budget work. So if you're tempted to pass over the cheaper cuts of meat for fear of how the family will react, turn a deaf ear to their protests and go right ahead (see page 11).

Take stuffed shoulder of lamb, for instance. All right, it's not the cheapest joint there is, but it's surprising how much further it will go when it's boned, rolled and stuffed with a special rosemary stuffing. And brisket of beef, cooked slowly until it's tender, can be just as delicious as the most expensive sirloin and no less nutritious.

Modern methods of intensive chicken farming have turned chicken into an everyday dish instead of the luxury it once was. Frozen chickens, in particular, are a good buy, the criticism that they have no taste is irrelevant if they're cooked with vegetables that do. The recipe for Spanish chicken, for example, with its peppers, olives and baby marrows, shows what can be done to disguise chicken left-overs (see page 52).

Chicken is useful, too, for disguising as something else. Why make a hole in the housekeeping money by buying veal escalopes when chicken breasts, beaten into tender fillets, are an equally tasty substitute? Served with herb butter at a dinner, they're an inexpensive method of gaining the praise of your guests.

Herrings in oatmeal

Fresh herrings – or indeed fresh mackerel – are wonderful served this way for supper.

Preparation time: 5 minutes
Cooking time: 10 minutes
Serves 4

4 herrings	1 oz (25 g) butter or margarine
2 level tbsp oatmeal	*Garnish*
½ level tsp dry mustard	Lemon slices
½ level tsp salt	Parsley

Ask the fishmonger to scale, clean and bone the herrings. Mix oatmeal mustard and salt together on a plate. Coat herrings with oatmeal mixture. Melt fat in frying pan. Fry herrings about 5 minutes each side. Drain on kitchen paper and garnish with lemon slices and parsley. Serve with brown bread and butter.

Haddock kedgeree

Smoked haddock is getting into the luxury class, so use golden fillets instead; their flavour is fine in a combined dish such as this one. Kipper fillets, too, are delicious served this way; but use only $\frac{1}{2}$ lb (225 g) as the flavour is stronger and omit the nutmeg. Best made and served straight away.

Preparation time: 10 minutes
Cooking time: 15 minutes
Oven: 325°F, 165°C, gas mark 3
Serves 6

$\frac{3}{4}$ lb (325 g) smoked haddock or golden fillets
1 oz (25 g) butter or margarine
6 oz (150 g) refined long-grain rice
Salt and pepper
1 tbsp chopped parsley
Pinch grated nutmeg
2 hard-boiled eggs

Put haddock in pan and cover with water. Simmer about 10 minutes or until haddock flakes easily. Remove from pan, reserving water. Remove and discard skin and bones from haddock. Flake and put into ovenproof dish; dot with butter or margarine. Cover with foil and keep warm in oven. Add rice to fish water and boil for about 12 minutes until just tender, adding a little more boiling water if necessary. Drain and add to the fish. Mix and season well with a little salt and pepper. Add parsley, then nutmeg and chopped hard-boiled eggs. Stir well and serve at once.

Cod steaks Provençal

Perhaps you've eaten halibut Provençal, a delicious French dish served by some restaurants. This is an easily prepared fish dish with a Provençal flavour to make at home. Skinned cod steaks or cutlets may be used.

Preparation time: 10 minutes
Cooking time: 50 minutes
Oven: 350°F, 180°C, gas mark 4
Serves 4

2 onions
2 cloves garlic
2 tbsp oil
1 tsp flour
7 oz (175 g) can tomatoes
Salt and pepper
Pinch sugar
1 tsp marjoram or oregano
4 cod steaks

Peel and slice onions and garlic; cook slowly in oil for 5 minutes and add the flour and canned tomato. Bring to the boil and season with salt, pepper, sugar and herbs. Put cod steaks in an ovenproof dish, spoon over the sauce, cover with a lid or foil and bake for 30 minutes or a little longer if fish is frozen.

To prepare in advance: Make the sauce up to 24 hours in advance and then spoon over the fish just before baking.
To freeze: Only the sauce is suitable for freezing. Defrost and spoon over the fish and bake.

Fish pie

Coley – also known as saithe – has a very good flavour and is inexpensive. In a fish pie its unpopular slightly grey colour is disguised. Sea bream, haddock or cod fillets may also be used. No extra vegetables to serve and no last-minute washing up with this tasty fish pie.

Preparation time: 15 minutes
Cooking time: 30 minutes
Serves 4

1 lb (500 g) coley	Salt and pepper
8 oz (225 g) peas	*Potato topping*
¾ pt (375 ml) milk	1½ lb (700 g) potatoes
1½ oz (40 g) butter	2 tbsp milk
1¼ oz (40 g) flour	Large knob butter
1 dsstsp parsley, chopped	Salt and pepper
2 hard-boiled eggs	2 tbsp cheese, grated

Skin and wash the coley, put in a pan with peas and milk and simmer gently for 10 minutes or until fish can be flaked with a fork. Tip into a bowl and set on one side. Rinse out the pan and then melt the butter. Remove from the heat and stir in flour. Add the milk strained from the fish. Return to the heat and bring to the boil. Remove any bones from fish and add to the sauce with peas, parsley, chopped hard-boiled eggs and seasoning.

In the meantime peel and boil potatoes. Drain, mash with milk and butter and then season. Pour hot fish into a dish and cover with mashed potatoes. Fork over the top to roughen and sprinkle on cheese; slip under the grill to brown.

To prepare in advance: Make up to 6 hours in advance, brown and reheat in a moderately hot oven for about 40 minutes.

Roast brisket

An excellent family slow roast. We have it at least one Sunday a month as the children prefer well-done, tender beef, as this is.

Preparation time: 3 minutes
Cooking time: 2 hours 30 minutes–3 hours 10 minutes

Oven: 425°F, 215°C, gas mark 7 to start, then see below
Serves 6

2½–3½ lb (1–1·5 kg) brisket, boned and rolled	1 stock cube
	Salt and pepper
	Water

Put meat in small meat tin, pour in 1 in (2·5 cm) water and add one stock cube. Season meat with salt and pepper. Cover with foil and roast covered at 425°F, 215°C, gas mark 7, for 20 minutes. Then lower oven to 300°F, 150°C, gas mark 2, for 40 minutes per lb (or 85 minutes per kg) of meat. Cook for further 30 minutes uncovered at 400°F, 200°C, gas mark 6, to finish browning potatoes and meat and to cook Yorkshire pudding. Make gravy with juices from meat and stock in meat tin.

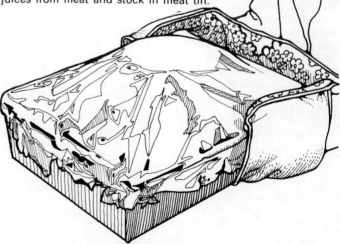

Roast stuffed lamb

Stuffings not only add to the flavour of the meat, they make it go further. Make this stuffing for pork too, but add sage instead of rosemary.

Preparation time: 15 minutes
Cooking time: 1½ hours
Oven: 375°F, 190°C, gas mark 5
Serves 6

1 shoulder of lamb, boned
Salt and pepper
1 oz (25 g) butter or margarine
1 small onion, chopped
4 rashers streaky bacon, rinded and chopped
2 oz (50 g) fresh white breadcrumbs
½ bunch watercress, chopped
1 garlic clove, crushed
½ level tsp dried rosemary

Open out shoulder and beat with a rolling pin to flatten slightly. Sprinkle inside of joint with seasoning. Melt fat in a pan, add onion and fry gently until soft. Add bacon and fry for 2 minutes. Remove from heat and stir in remaining ingredients, checking seasoning. Spread stuffing over meat and roll up firmly, tying with fine string at 1 in (2·5 cm) intervals. Place on a rack in meat tin and roast, allowing 30 minutes per lb (65 minutes per kg). Serve sliced with gravy made in the usual way with the juices from the pan.

To prepare in advance: Make stuffing, wrap in foil and keep in the refrigerator for up to 24 hours; stuff the joint on the day.

Chicken with lemon sauce

Boiling fowls cost considerably less per pound than roasting chicken. They can be rather fatty, so it's essential to remove fat from the stock by skimming it off with a large spoon and then absorbing the last bit with a piece of absorbent kitchen paper. The flavour of this dish is really strong lemon; add a little fresh chopped tarragon before serving if you have some.

Preparation time: 30 minutes
Cooking time: 2–4 hours
Serves 6

4 lb (2 kg) boiling fowl and giblets	Bouquet garni
	Salt and pepper
2 lemons thinly peeled, rind and juice	*Sauce*
	2 oz (50 g) butter or margarine
2 onions, quartered	2 oz (50 g) flour
1 carrot, quartered	½ pt (250 ml) milk
2 sprigs parsley	Fresh parsley, chopped

Rinse the chicken in cold water and stuff the bird with the rind of half a lemon, the giblets and a sprig of parsley. Put into a saucepan with the rest of the lemon rind, onion, carrot, bouquet garni, salt and pepper. Cover with water and simmer until tender, depending on the age of the bird. When cooked take out the bird, remove the lemon rind, giblets and parsley; keep hot while preparing the sauce.

Skim off fat from the stock and strain off ½ pt (250 ml). The remainder can be used for soup. Melt the butter, blend in the flour and cook this roux (see page 14) over a low heat for 2 minutes, stirring frequently. Blend in the milk, a little at a time, away from the heat. Return the pan to the heat and bring to boiling point, stirring all the time. Simmer until the sauce has thickened, then add the stock and lemon juice, lastly the seasoning. Place the bird on a serving dish and cover with the sauce. Sprinkle generously with chopped parsley.

To prepare in advance: Cook up to 24 hours ahead, cover and put in the refrigerator. Reheat and serve piping hot.
To freeze: Chicken with lemon sauce freezes well.

Chicken escalopes

Chicken is always a reasonably cheap buy, whereas fillet of veal for escalopes is very expensive. For this recipe buy a wing joint that includes the breast; beat the breast meat out and you have a tender fillet for frying.

Preparation time: 20 minutes
Cooking time: 10 minutes
Serves 6

Herbed butter
3 oz (75 g) salted butter or margarine, softened
2 tsp lemon juice
2 tsp chopped parsley
1 tsp chopped fresh tarragon
Escalopes
6 wing joints, including breasts
1 oz (25 g) seasoned flour
1 egg, beaten
3 rounded tbsp brown breadcrumbs
Oil for deep frying

Blend together all ingredients for herbed butter. Place on piece of foil and form into a sausage shape; roll up in foil and chill.

Remove skin and bones from chicken joints with sharp knife, keeping each joint whole. Trim any small pieces of chicken off to make an even shape. Place joints between two sheets of damp greaseproof paper and flatten with a rolling pin. Coat joints with flour, then egg and breadcrumbs. Heat oil in large pan, add joints and fry. Drain on kitchen paper and serve with slices of herbed butter.

To prepare in advance: Prepare chicken, egg and breadcrumbs. Cover and keep in refrigerator for up to 24 hours before cooking. Make herbed butter at the same time.

American chicken

If you enjoy a sweet taste with chicken, you'll enjoy this recipe. Serve with rice or noodles rather than potatoes. If preferred, leave chicken on the bone.

Preparation time: 15 minutes
Cooking time: 20–30 minutes
Serves 4

4 roasting chicken joints
$\frac{1}{2}$ oz (15 g) seasoned flour
3 tbsp oil
1 small green pepper, seeded and chopped
$\frac{1}{2}$ lb (225 g) new carrots, scraped
8 oz (225 g) can pineapple pieces
10 oz (275 g) can condensed tomato soup
Salt and pepper

Remove flesh from chicken joints in fairly large pieces; discard skin and bone. Toss chicken in seasoned flour. Heat oil in large pan and fry chicken pieces. Remove chicken from pan and drain. Add green pepper and carrots to pan; fry for 5 minutes. Add remaining flour and cook for 1 minute. Blend in pineapple pieces, juice and tomato soup. Bring to boiling point, stirring. Return chicken to pan; check seasoning and simmer.

To prepare in advance: Cook chicken dish, cover and cool. Keep in refrigerator for up to 24 hours.

Chicken foil parcels

These make a good supper dish and teenagers and older children love having their own parcel to undo. Serve with rice or mashed potato. If fresh tomatoes are expensive, use canned tomatoes including juice.

Preparation time: 15 minutes
Cooking time: 1 hour
Oven: 325°F, 160°C, gas mark 3
Serves 4

4 chicken joints
1 oz (25 g) seasoned flour
1 oz (25 g) dripping
1 large onion, chopped
1 lb (500 g) tomatoes, skinned and quartered
1 clove garlic, crushed
$\frac{1}{4}$ level tsp mixed herbs
Salt and pepper

Toss chicken in seasoned flour. Heat dripping in frying pan, add chicken joints and brown quickly, turning once. Remove chicken joints from pan and place each on 10 in (25 cm) square of heavy-duty foil or on double thickness ordinary foil. Add onion to pan and cook until soft. Blend in remaining flour and cook 1 minute. Add tomatoes, garlic and herbs and simmer for 2 minutes. Check seasoning and spoon sauce over chicken joints. Wrap each one firmly in foil and put on baking tray to cook.

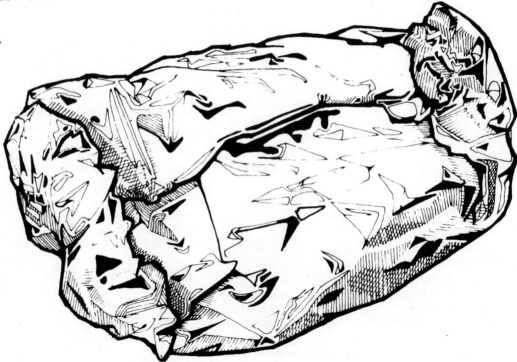

Pork loaf

This goes well with salad meals and pickles and is also very manageable to take on a picnic. Instead of mushrooms, mushroom stalks can be used if you see them in the greengrocer's. The remains of the loaf can be used as a sandwich filling.

Preparation time: 30 minutes
Cooking time: 2½ hours
Oven: 350°F, 175°C, gas mark 4
Serves 4

½ lemon, thinly sliced
1¼ lb (600 g) pig's liver
½ lb (225 g) fat pork
½ lb (225 g) mushrooms
1 clove garlic
1 medium onion
4 tbsp brandy (optional)
1 oz (25 g) flour
2 eggs, beaten
1½ level tsp salt
½ level tsp pepper
½ level tsp allspice
½ level tsp dried sage
¼ level tsp ground mace
3 tbsp top of milk
2 tomatoes, sliced

Grease a 2 lb (1 kg) loaf tin with lard and line base with lemon slices. Mince together liver, pork, mushrooms, garlic and onion. Stir in remaining ingredients and mix well. Turn into a prepared loaf tin and cover with a lid or foil. Place in a meat tin half-filled with warm water and bake. Leave to cool in tin, then turn out on to a serving dish and garnish with tomato. Serve in slices with salad.

To prepare in advance: Turn out, wrap in plastic wrap or foil and keep in refrigerator for up to four days.
To freeze: Pork loaf freezes well.

Beefburgers au poivre

Buy a good brand of frozen beefburgers and make them more exciting by serving in this way. The peppered beefburgers are each served on a pâté-covered croûte, then topped with a whole tomato and garnished with parsley.

Preparation time: 10 minutes
Cooking time: 20 minutes
Serves 6

6 slices white bread
4 tbsp oil
1 oz (25 g) butter or margarine
6 frozen beefburgers, thawed
Coarsely ground black pepper
1 oz (25 g) pâté de foie truffé
6 small tomatoes, skinned
Chopped parsley

Cut a 4 in (10 cm) circle from each slice of bread. Heat oil in frying pan and add butter or margarine. When this has melted, add bread croûtes to pan, fry until golden brown, turning once. Drain croûtes on kitchen paper.

Season beefburgers liberally with pepper and add to pan. Fry gently for 7 minutes, turning once. Cut pâté in six wedges and spread one on each croûte. Place a beefburger on top of each croûte and keep hot. Grill tomatoes lightly and place one on top of each beefburger; top with parsley.

To prepare in advance: Fry croûtes, cool and wrap in foil. Skin tomatoes and refrigerate. Thaw beefburgers also in refrigerator. This may be done up to 24 hours ahead.

Skinny Liz salad

A refreshing salad for a slimming lunch.

Preparation time: 15 minutes
Serves 4

8 oz (225 g) cottage cheese
4 spring onions, chopped
¼ level tsp dried dill
¼ level tsp freshly ground black pepper
4 oz (100 g) shelled prawns
1 small green pepper,
seeded and sliced
2 heads chicory
1 lemon, cut in 8 wedges

Blend together cottage cheese, spring onion, dill and pepper. Chop most of the prawns coarsely and add to cheese mixture. Arrange green pepper rings and chicory leaves on four individual plates. Pile cheese mixture on top and garnish with remaining prawns. Serve with lemon wedges.

To prepare in advance: Prepare up to an hour or so beforehand. Cover and keep in the refrigerator.

Chapter 5
One-pot meat cooking

This is every busy person's dream — and for that matter every washer-up's as well. It's the meal that is cooked in one pot — sauce-pan, casserole or pie dish — so that once the initial preparation is finished all you have to do is to sit back and wait for it to cook.

Usually the actual cooking time is nice and slow, which gives you time to nip to the shops or collect the children from school. And if you go out to work full time and want to have dinner at the civilised time of 7.30 instead of some time after 9 o'clock, you can prepare the dish in the morning, place it in the oven before you leave for work and set the time switch to turn on the oven an hour or so before you come home.

Best of all, the long, slow cooking enables you to use cheap cuts of meat that are too tough to grill or roast.

Beef casserole

This is an ideal meal to put in the oven first thing in the morning and go out shopping. All you have to do when you come back is to toss in the prepared vegetables.

Preparation time: 20 minutes
Cooking time: 3 hours
Oven: 325°F, 160°C, gas mark 3
Serves 6

1 oz (25 g) dripping
1½ lb (675 g) stewing steak in 1 in (2.5 cm) pieces
1 oz (25 g) flour
1 pt (500 ml) water
1 beef stock cube
Salt and pepper
2 bay leaves
¼ level tsp dried thyme
4 medium potatoes, peeled and halved
½ lb (225 g) carrots, scraped and quartered
2 large leeks, sliced

Heat dripping in pan, add meat and cook quickly until browned. Add flour, blend in water and turn into a 2½ pt (1.5 l) casserole. Add stock cube, seasoning and herbs and cook for 2½ hours. Add vegetables and cook for further ½ hour or until vegetables are tender. Remove bay leaves and check seasoning.

To prepare in advance: Cook, cover and cool. Keep in refrigerator for up to 24 hours.
To freeze: Beef casserole freezes well.

Hungarian beef goulash

Goulash is a lovely dish in winter. All the vegetables are cooked, which means there are no last-minute potatoes to do. Increase the paprika if your family are goulash addicts. The salt pork adds to the saltiness of the stew, so go easy on the salt and check seasoning and add more if need be at the end of cooking.

Preparation time: 25 minutes
Cooking time: 2½ hours
Oven: 300°F, 155°C, gas mark 2
Serves 6

1½ lb (675 g) chuck beef	1 oz (25 g) flour
4 oz (100 g) salt pork	2 level tbsp paprika
1 large onion	1 pt (500 ml) water
6 small onions	1 beef stock cube
12 small potatoes	2 bay leaves
6 small carrots	Salt and pepper
½ oz (15 g) lard	

Cut beef in 1 in (2·5 cm) pieces. Cut pork in ½ in (1·5 cm) pieces. Chop large onion. Peel small vegetables and keep under water until needed. Melt lard in pan and fry pork slowly until brown. Remove from pan and place in 2½ pt (1·5 l) ovenproof dish. Add beef and chopped onion to pan. Cook quickly until brown and put in casserole. Blend flour with fat in pan and cook 1 minute. Stir in paprika, then water and stock cube. Bring to boil, stirring. Simmer 2 minutes. Add bay leaves and little seasoning, then pour sauce over meat. Cover and cook for 1½ hours; add vegetables and cook for further 1 hour. Remove bay leaves before serving.

To prepare in advance: Completely cook, cool and keep in refrigerator for up to 24 hours. Reheat.
To freeze: Undercook a little then freeze.

Pot-au-feu bourgeois

There is no salt mentioned in this recipe as the knuckle of bacon could well be salty and therefore flavour the beef. Check seasoning at the end of the cooking and add salt if need be then. Goes well with purée potatoes.

Preparation time: 20 minutes
Cooking time: 3 hours
Serves 6

1½ lb (675 g) chuck steak, in 1 in (2·5 cm) cubes
⅛ tsp pepper
½ oz (15 g) flour
2 oz (50 g) dripping
2 onions, chopped
1 carrot, diced

4 sticks celery, chopped
½ lb (225 g) piece knuckle bacon
¼ pt (125 ml) burgundy or cider
⅓ pt (175 ml) water

Toss the meat in peppered flour. Melt dripping in pan, add meat and fry quickly until brown. Remove meat from pan and drain on kitchen paper. Add vegetables to the pan, fry until brown. Return meat to pan with bacon, wine or cider and water. Cover and simmer very slowly until tender. Take bacon from pan, remove lean meat from bone and return to pan. Discard fat and bone. Skim off any remaining fat and check seasoning.

To prepare in advance: Cook, cover and cool. Refrigerate and reheat. Use within 48 hours.

Liver casserole

Young ox liver can be absolutely delicious, but it *must* be young; otherwise use fresh pig's liver or the more expensive calf's liver. Best made and served on the same day as reheating liver can make it hard.

Preparation time: 15 minutes
Cooking time: 2 hours
Oven: 300°F, 150°C, gas mark 2
Serves 6

1 lb (500 g) young ox liver, thinly sliced
1 oz (25 g) seasoned flour
2 oz (50 g) lard
½ lb (225 g) onions, thinly sliced
¾ pt (375 ml) water
1 beef stock cube
1 tbsp soy sauce
2 level tbsp tomato purée
1 tbsp Worcester sauce
6 rashers streaky bacon, rinded
Salt and pepper

Soak liver for 10 minutes in bowl of salted water, then drain dry on kitchen paper. Toss in seasoned flour. Heat 1 oz (25 g) lard in large pan, add liver and fry quickly until browned, turning once. Remove from pan and add remaining lard and onions. Fry onions slowly until soft and pale golden, blend in any remaining flour and cook for 1 minute. Add water to pan and bring to boiling point, stirring. Remove from heat, add liver and all remaining ingredients except bacon. Check seasoning, then turn into 1½ pt (1 l) ovenproof casserole, cover and cook until tender. Just before serving, grill bacon rashers until crisp; use as garnish.

Spiced beef casserole with dumplings

Old-fashioned dumplings are lovely when there's lots of well-flavoured gravy to dunk them in. They help to make a meal more satisfying on a cold day.

Preparation time: 20 minutes
Cooking time: 2 hours
Oven: 325°F, 160°C, gas mark 3
Serves 6

1½ lb (675 g) chuck steak, in 1 in (2·5 cm) cubes
1 oz (25 g) seasoned flour
1 oz (25 g) dripping
1 large onion, sliced
1 pt (500 ml) water
4 level tbsp tomato purée
Pinch dried basil
Salt and pepper

Dumplings
4 oz (100 g) self-raising flour
1 level tsp salt
4 level tbsp shredded suet
1 level tbsp horseradish sauce
1 tbsp chopped parsley
3–4 tbsp cold water

Toss steak in seasoned flour. Heat dripping in large pan, add onion and cook gently until browned. Add meat and fry 5 minutes, then blend in water, tomato purée and basil. Bring to boiling point, stirring. Turn mixture into 3 pt (1·75 l) ovenproof casserole, cover and cook. Check seasoning.

Sift together flour and salt for dumplings, then add suet. Blend horseradish sauce, parsley and water together. Blend with flour to make a soft dough. Shape into eight balls and cook, covered, in casserole for last 45 minutes of cooking time.

To prepare in advance: Cook, cover and cool; keep in the refrigerator for up to 24 hours. On reheating, the dumplings lose a little of their lightness.

Winter lamb hotpot

A delicious family-lunch casserole. Get it in the oven early in the morning and it cooks itself. For brown potatoes, lift the lid off for the last half hour of cooking. If you want another vegetable to serve with the hotpot, braise some carrots in the oven at the same time.

Preparation time: 25 minutes
Cooking time: 2½ hours
Oven: 350°F, 180°C, gas mark 4
Serves 4

2 lb (1 kg) middle neck or scrag end of lamb
½ oz (15 kg) flour
Salt and pepper
1½ lb (675 g) potatoes
½ lb (225 g) onions
2 lamb's kidneys
¼ lb (100 g) button mushrooms
¾ pt (375 ml) stock or water
½ oz (15 g) butter or margarine

Cut lamb into even-sized chops and pieces. Mix flour with salt and pepper and toss meat in it. Peel potatoes and cut into ¼ in (0·5 cm) thick slices. Peel and slice onion; skin, core and quarter kidneys. Wash, dry and slice mushrooms. Put meat, onion, kidney, and mushrooms in casserole, arranging potato slices on top. Pour on stock. Place small pieces of butter or margarine on top of potatoes. Cover dish and cook.

Braised oxtail

An oxtail takes long, slow cooking and the meat should come easily off the bone when it's done. Skim any surplus fat off the casserole before straining the sauce. In our family we give everyone a soup spoon to finish up every drop of the rich, flavoursome gravy.

Preparation time: 15 minutes
Cooking time: 4 hours
Serves 6

3 lb (1·5 kg) oxtail, in pieces
2 oz (50 g) lard or dripping
2 onions, chopped
2 large carrots, chopped
$\frac{1}{2}$ head celery, chopped
2 rashers streaky bacon, chopped
1 oz (25 g) flour

2 bay leaves
3 sprigs parsley
6 peppercorns
Salt
2 pt (1 l) water
2 beef stock cubes
Gravy browning

Trim off any excess fat from the oxtail joints. Heat fat in pan, add oxtail and brown quickly on all sides, then remove from pan. Add vegetables and bacon to the pan, cook gently for 5 minutes. Blend in flour, cook 1 minute then return oxtail to pan with remaining ingredients, except browning. Cover and simmer for 4 hours, or until meat can be removed easily from the bones. Arrange on serving dish and keep hot. Reduce stock to $\frac{3}{4}$ pt (375 ml) by rapid boiling; remove parsley stalks and bay leaves, check seasoning, add a little gravy browning, then strain over oxtail.

To prepare in advance: Cook completely, cool in refrigerator for up to 48 hours.
To freeze: Braised oxtail freezes well but is bulky and takes up more room in the freezer than the normal casserole.

Swedish meatballs

As meat gets more expensive I'm always trying to find different ways with mince. This is a great favourite — the onion gravy is really rich.

Preparation time: 20 minutes
Cooking time: 35 minutes
Makes 16

$\frac{3}{4}$ lb (325 g) minced beef
2 oz (50 g) fresh white breadcrumbs
1 egg
Salt and pepper
$\frac{1}{4}$ level tsp dried marjoram
Sauce
1 oz (25 g) dripping
$\frac{1}{2}$ lb (225 g) onions
1 oz (25 g) flour
$\frac{1}{2}$ pt (250 ml) beef stock
1 tbsp tomato ketchup
1 dsstsp Worcester sauce
$\frac{1}{4}$ tsp gravy browning

Place beef, breadcrumbs, egg, seasoning and herbs in a bowl and mix well. Turn out on to a floured board and shape into sixteen balls. Heat the dripping in a frying pan and fry the meatballs until brown all over; lift out on to a plate. Peel and slice the onions, put in the pan and cook for 2–3 minutes. Stir in the flour, add the stock and bring to the boil, stirring. Add the ketchup, Worcester sauce and browning. Season to taste. Return the balls to the pan, cover and cook slowly for 30 minutes. Turn on to a warm serving dish and serve.

To prepare in advance: Cook and cool up to 24 hours ahead; put in refrigerator. Reheat when needed.
To freeze: Swedish meatballs freeze well.

Beefburger toad

Home-made beefburgers are easy and twice as nice as bought ones. They keep their shape well and go well with a large portion of crisp batter.

Preparation time: 20 minutes
Cooking time: 35–40 minutes
Oven: 425°F, 215°C, gas mark 7
Serves 4–6

½ lb (225 g) minced beef
½ lb (225 g) sausage meat
Salt and pepper
½ level tsp mixed dried herbs
Knob of dripping
Batter
4 oz (100 g) plain flour
1 level tsp salt
1 egg, beaten
½ pt (250 ml) milk and water mixed

Mix mince, sausage meat, seasoning and herbs together. Shape into six round beefburgers and lightly coat with flour. Melt a knob of dripping in a roasting tin 7 in × 11 in (18 cm × 28 cm). Add beefburgers.

  Sieve flour and salt into a mixing bowl and add beaten egg, milk and water. Mix to a smooth batter. Pour the batter over the beefburgers and bake in the oven until well risen, crisp and golden brown.

To prepare in advance: Make beefburgers and batter up to 24 hours ahead. Cover beefburgers and put batter in jug; refrigerate until needed.

Stuffed cabbage rolls

The Italians stuff vine leaves because they have them to hand. Cabbage leaves, I think, are even nicer stuffed. Serve them with onion sauce (see recipe on page 48). A mixture of half beef and half pork is best; otherwise use raw minced beef. If you like, pour the onion sauce around the cabbage rolls during cooking instead of the cabbage water.

Preparation time: 25 minutes
Cooking time: 1¼ hours
Oven: 350°F, 180°C, gas mark 4
Serves 6

1 medium Savoy cabbage
Salt and pepper
½ lb (225 g) leg of pork, raw
½ lb (225 g) chuck beef, raw
1 slice bread
2–3 tbsp top of the milk
1 egg, beaten

Remove twelve leaves carefully from cabbage so they remain whole. Cook in boiling, salted water for 2 minutes. Drain thoroughly, reserving water, and remove thickest part of the stem. Mince pork and beef finely. Mash bread with milk and plenty of seasoning. Bind mixture together with beaten egg. Form into twelve rissole shapes and put one on each cabbage leaf. Roll each leaf up to form a parcel and arrange in ovenproof dish. Pour around a little of the cabbage water. Cover and cook. Serve with onion sauce.

To prepare in advance: Make each cabbage roll, place in ovenproof dish, cover and put in the refrigerator up to 12 hours ahead. Then cook and make sauce.

Sausage risotto

This recipe is just for sausages, but if you've had a roast chicken with sausages you could use any left-over meat trimmings from the bird with the sausages. And the chicken liver, chopped and cooked, would add to the flavour. Best to make the risotto just before it is needed.

Preparation time: 15 minutes
Cooking time: 15 minutes
Serves 4

5 oz (125 g) long-grain rice
Salt
½ lb (225 g) pork chipolata sausages
1 rasher streaky bacon
½ oz (15 g) lard
7 oz (200 g) can tomatoes
Pepper
Chopped parsley

Boil rice in plenty of salted water for 12 minutes or until tender. Refresh in hot water. Twist each sausage link into two small sausages and prick. Derind bacon and cut into small pieces. Melt lard and slowly fry sausages until pale brown. Add bacon and cook 2 minutes. Stir in rice and drained tomatoes. Blend well until piping hot. Season and add chopped parsley.

Sausage, onion and tomato casserole

A favourite of mine for putting in the oven at great speed before rushing out shopping on a Saturday morning. Ideally you should turn the sausages once so that they brown on both sides.

Preparation time: 10 minutes
Cooking time: 1¼–1½ hours
Oven: 375°F, 195°C, gas mark 5
Serves 4

1 clove garlic
2 onions
2 sticks celery
2–3 medium potatoes
15 oz (475 g) can tomatoes
2 level tsp dry mustard
½ tsp sugar
Salt and pepper
8 large pork sausages

Butter a 2 pt (1 l) ovenproof casserole. Chop or crush garlic. Peel onions and slice into rings. Slice celery ¼ in (0·5 cm) thick; peel and slice potatoes ¼ in (0·5 cm) thick. Combine all vegetables including tomatoes and juice, but save 2 tbsp juice. Blend mustard with juice. Add to vegetables with sugar, salt and pepper. Turn into casserole, arranging sausages on top. Cover for last part of cooking if sausages are getting too brown.

Steak, kidney and mushroom loaf pudding

Ideal for a hungry family.

Preparation time: 30 minutes
Cooking time: 2¾ hours
Oven: 325°F, 160°C, gas mark 3
Serves 6

1 oz (25 g) lard
1 lb (500 g) skirt beef in 1 in (2·5 cm) dice
¾ lb (325 g) ox kidney in ½ in (1·5 cm) dice
1 oz (25 g) seasoned flour
1 large onion, chopped
¾ pt (375 ml) water
1 beef stock cube
Salt and pepper
4 oz (100 g) mushrooms, sliced
Suet pastry
8 oz (225 g) self-raising flour
½ level tsp salt
4 oz (100 g) shredded suet
About 8 tbsp cold water

Heat lard in pan. Toss beef and kidney in seasoned flour, add to pan and fry quickly until browned. Remove meat from pan, add onion and cook until soft. Blend in any remaining flour and cook for 1 minute. Add water and stock cube. Bring to boil and simmer for 2 minutes. Return meat to pan, season, cover and simmer for 1 hour. Add mushrooms and cool.

Put flour, salt and suet in bowl. Blend in water to make soft dough. Grease a 2 lb (1 kg) loaf tin. Roll out two-thirds of pastry and use to line base and sides of tin. Drain meat mixture, reserving liquid. Put meat in tin with half of the cooking liquor. Moisten pastry edges with water, cover with remaining pastry, press edges together, cover with greased foil and bake. Reheat remaining liquor and serve as gravy.

To prepare in advance: Cook steak and kidney, cover and refrigerate for up to 24 hours. Make pastry and loaf three hours before serving.

Chapter 6
Cooking with left-overs

In the 'good' old days, a housewife usually managed to make the Sunday joint last well into the week — cold on Monday, hash on Tuesday, mince on Wednesday, rissoles on Thursday.

Today, well, you're lucky if that miserable apology of a joint is fit to be seen on a Monday, let alone eaten. So it pays in the long run to buy the largest joint you can afford, since the bigger the joint the less the shrinkage there will be in the original cooking and the more meat to use up later.

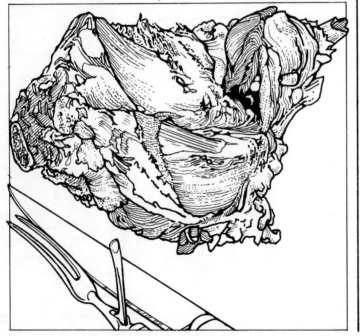

Spanish chicken

An unusual and colourful way of using up left-over chicken or turkey; quick and easy to prepare, it's a useful dish, especially at Christmas. In the summer 1 pound (500 g) of cheap, fresh tomatoes could be used (skin and slice them first).

Preparation time: 15 minutes
Cooking time: 25 minutes
Serves 4

2 large Spanish onions
1 clove garlic
2 tbsp chicken or turkey dripping or oil
1 dsstp chopped parsley
14 oz (400 g) can tomatoes
6 stuffed Spanish olives
12 oz (350 g) chicken or turkey, cooked and cut up
Pinch sugar
Salt and black pepper
6 extra olives for decoration

Peel and slice the onions and garlic; fry in oil or dripping until golden brown, turning occasionally. Add the chopped parsley and put on one side to keep hot. Add the tomatoes and the sliced olives to the pan and cook quickly for about 5 minutes until the tomatoes are reduced to a thickish sauce. Season with sugar, salt and pepper and stir in the meat cut in large pieces. Reheat and serve in a dish topped with the onions and decorated with olives.

To prepare in advance: Make up to 6 hours in advance, cover the dish and reheat for 25 minutes in a moderate oven.
To freeze: left-over chicken or turkey may be frozen then used for this dish, but the meat is best not refrozen a second time once you have prepared this dish.

Lamb moussaka with yogurt topping

Moussaka is one of the classic recipes of Greece. This one has added potato slices to eke out the aubergines, which are expensive.

Preparation time: 35 minutes
Cooking time: 1 hour 20 minutes
Oven: 375°F, 190°C, gas mark 5
Serves 6

2 tbsp oil
1 large onion, chopped
1 level tsp rosemary
1 lb (500 g) cooked lamb, minced
Salt
Freshly ground black pepper
$\frac{3}{4}$ lb (325 g) potatoes, thinly sliced
2 aubergines cut into $\frac{1}{4}$ in (0·5 cm) slices
1 lb (500 g) tomatoes, skinned and sliced
Cheese sauce
1 oz (25 g) butter or margarine
1 oz (25 g) flour
$\frac{1}{2}$ pt (250 ml) milk
2 oz (50 g) cheese, grated
$\frac{1}{2}$ level tsp powdered nutmeg
$\frac{1}{4}$ level tsp garlic powder (optional)
$\frac{1}{4}$ level tsp each salt and pepper
Yogurt topping
1 egg
1 oz (25 g) flour
$\frac{1}{4}$ level tsp powdered mustard
5 oz (125 g) natural yogurt
Salt and pepper
Paprika to garnish

Heat oil in frying pan, add onion and cook gently 2–3 minutes. Add rosemary, then minced lamb and brown quickly for 5 minutes, stirring continuously with a fork. Season.

To make cheese sauce, melt fat in saucepan, stir in flour and cook for 2–3 minutes. Remove from heat and gradually stir in milk. Bring to boil and cook for 2–3 minutes, stirring continuously. Stir in cheese, nutmeg and garlic powder. Season.

Place half the potato slices in the bottom of a deep 8 in (20 cm) diameter casserole. Add half of each of the other ingredients, i.e. onion and lamb, aubergines, tomatoes, cheese sauce, in layers, seasoning each layer of vegetables. Repeat, finishing with layer of potato. Cook for 1 hour.

To make yogurt topping, blend egg, flour and mustard. Stir in yogurt and seasoning. Spoon on to moussaka. Continue cooking for 20 minutes. Serve sprinkled with paprika pepper.

To prepare in advance: As raw potatoes discolour, it's best to make and cook this dish simultaneously. If need be, the dish could be cooked completely, cooled and then reheated.

Beef croquettes

Call them rissoles or what you like; they taste good and make the most of the last trimmings off the Sunday roast. Make sure they are well seasoned.

Preparation time: 15 minutes
Cooking time: 5 minutes
Serves 4

2 oz (50 g) butter or margarine
2 oz (50 g) flour
1 beef stock cube
½ pt (250 ml) milk
8 oz (225 g) cooked beef, finely chopped
1 egg, beaten
1 tbsp chopped parsley
Salt and pepper
For coating
1 oz (25 g) flour
1 egg, beaten
Browned breadcrumbs
Fat or oil for deep frying

Make a roux (see page 14) with the fat and flour; cook 1 minute. Crumble cube in milk, then blend with roux and bring to boiling point. Simmer 2 minutes, stirring well. Remove from heat and add chopped beef. Stir in egg, parsley and seasoning, then leave until cold. Divide mixture in eight and make into cylinder shapes. Coat each with flour, then egg and crumbs. Leave in refrigerator 30 minutes. Heat fat or oil, add croquettes and fry about 4 minutes until golden brown. Drain on kitchen paper and serve at once.

To prepare in advance: Make croquettes, coat in egg and breadcrumbs; keep in refrigerator for up to 24 hours.
To freeze: Make, but don't fry. Freeze for not longer than one month. After thawing, coat with second layer of egg and breadcrumbs before frying. This gives a thicker crisp crust and prevents the croquettes bursting.

Curried beef with hard-boiled eggs

This same recipe can be made with most left-over meat from the roast, the best being beef, lamb and chicken. If you have less meat left, add more eggs.

Preparation time: 20 minutes
Cooking time: 20 minutes
Serves 4

1 oz (25 g) lard
1 onion, finely sliced
1 level tbsp curry powder, or to taste
½ pt (250 ml) water
1 beef stock cube
8 oz (225 g) cooked beef in ½ in (1 cm) pieces
Juice of ½ lemon
2 tbsp chutney
Salt and pepper
2 hard-boiled eggs

Melt fat in pan, add onion and cook slowly until soft. Add curry powder and fry 1 minute. Add water and bring to boiling point, stirring, then add all remaining ingredients except eggs. Cover and simmer 15 minutes. Shell eggs and cut in quarters. Just before serving, add eggs to beef mixture. Serve with plain boiled rice, peeled and sliced cucumber, sultanas, sliced banana and coconut.

To prepare in advance: Hard boil eggs and make sauce up to 48 hours ahead, storing in the refrigerator. Prepare garnishes and rice just before the meal.

Chicken pilaff

When the cooked chicken or even turkey gets on its last legs and there is just 8 oz (225 g) or so left on the bird, this is an ideal way of spinning it out. And if there's even less meat left, add some sliced cooked sausages when the rice is added. Best made and eaten on the same day.

Preparation time: 15 minutes
Cooking time: 55 minutes
Serves 4

1 oz (25 g) butter or margarine
1 onion, sliced
1 small green pepper, seeded and sliced
1 garlic clove, crushed
½ oz (15 g) flour
8 oz (225 g) can tomatoes
½ cucumber, peeled and sliced
4 level tbsp tomato purée
2 tsp Worcester sauce
Pinch ground cloves
Pinch chilli powder
Pinch dried basil
Salt and pepper
½ pt (250 ml) water
8 oz (225 g) cooked chicken, diced
6 oz (150 g) long-grain rice
1 tbsp chopped parsley

Heat fat in a pan, add onion, green pepper and garlic; cook gently until soft. Blend in flour and cook for 1 minute. Add all ingredients except chicken, rice and parsley. Cover and simmer 45 minutes; add chicken and cook further 10 minutes. Cook rice in boiling, salted water for 12 minutes or until just tender. Drain rice, mix with parsley and spoon round edge of serving dish. Pile chicken mixture in centre.

Chicken pie

An excellent way of serving chicken a second time round. If there's not quite enough meat, add sliced and cooked root vegetables and a few uncooked frozen peas to spin things out.

Preparation time: 30 minutes
Cooking time: 30 minutes
Oven: 425°F, 215°C, gas mark 7
Serves 4

Filling
8 oz (225 g) cooked chicken
4 oz (100 g) cooked bacon or ham
2 oz (50 g) butter or margarine
4 oz (100 g) button mushrooms
1 oz (25 g) flour
½ pt (250 ml) milk
Pinch ground mace
Salt and pepper
Juice ½ lemon
Pastry
13 oz (375 g) packet rough puff pastry, thawed
Beaten egg or milk for glazing

Cut chicken and bacon in small pieces. Melt 1 oz (25 g) fat in pan and fry mushrooms 1 minute. Remove mushrooms, melt remaining fat in pan, blend in flour and cook 1 minute. Remove from heat; stir in milk. Bring sauce to boiling point, stirring. Simmer 2 minutes. Add mace, salt, pepper, lemon juice. Put chicken, bacon and mushrooms into sauce and mix well. Leave to cool in a 1½ pt (1 l) ovenproof dish.

Roll out pastry thinly and use to cover dish. Make pastry trimmings into leaves for decoration and brush pie lightly with glaze. Cook until well risen and golden brown.

To prepare in advance: Make but don't bake; put in the refrigerator up to 12 hours beforehand.

Chapter 7
Pasta, cheese and eggs

With today's more sophisticated tastes, there are plenty of recipes from abroad with which to ring the changes on the week's meals. And remember that meat is not essential *every* day — eggs and cheese may be used in a number of ways to provide all the protein a family needs.

Lasagne

Maybe you've had lasagne in Italian restaurants on holiday; it really is delicious. Using a can of minced beef speeds up the operation when making the meat base; but if you prefer to make your own, use the spaghetti bolognese meat sauce recipe on page 59. Lasagne is excellent for entertaining and needs to be served only with a green salad. Gruyère is best in this recipe but well-flavoured Cheddar will do.

Preparation time: 30 minutes
Cooking time: 40 minutes
Oven: 350°F, 180°C, gas mark 4
Serves 6

Meat sauce
15 oz (475 g) can minced beef
¼ level tsp garlic powder
4 tbsp tomato purée
8 oz (225 g) can tomatoes
Pinch mixed herbs
1 tsp sugar
⅛ level tsp black pepper
½ level tsp salt
White sauce
1 oz (25 g) butter or margarine
1 oz (25 g) flour
¾ pt (375 ml) milk
Salt and pepper
Lasagne
4 pt (2·25 l) water
1 tbsp salad oil
½ level tbsp salt
¼ lb (100 g) lasagne
6 oz (150 g) Gruyère or strong Cheddar
1 oz (25 g) grated Parmesan

Turn can of mince into bowl. Stir in other ingredients, including liquid from tomatoes. For white sauce, make roux (page 14) with fat and flour. Blend in milk and bring to boil, stirring. Simmer 2 minutes and season with salt and pepper. Cover sauce and keep hot.

Prepare lasagne. Boil water with oil and salt. Place lasagne in water one piece at a time. Boil for 8 minutes or until just tender. Drain, rinse with cold water and leave on a clean, damp tea towel to prevent pieces sticking together. Grate Gruyère cheese. Assemble dish in layers in shallow fireproof dish, starting with layer of meat sauce, then pasta, white sauce and then some cheese. Sprinkle with remaining Gruyère cheese and then Parmesan. Cook until golden brown.

To prepare in advance: Complete, but don't bake. Cover and put in refrigerator for up to 12 hours.
To freeze: An excellent recipe for freezing; freeze before baking.

Spaghetti bake with peppers

This is a good supper dish made of layered spaghetti, minced meat mixture and tomatoes. It's not unlike lasagne but without the cheese sauce.

Preparation time: 25 minutes
Cooking time: 40 minutes
Oven: 350°F, 175°C, gas mark 4
Serves 4

6 oz (150 g) spaghetti
Salt
1 onion
1 green pepper
½ oz (15 g) lard
1 lb (500 g) minced beef
Pepper
¼ level tsp dried thyme
15 oz (475 g) can tomatoes
1 oz (25 g) dry matured Cheddar cheese, grated

Cook spaghetti in boiling, salted water for 12 minutes or until just tender. Drain and put on one side. Peel onion and chop finely. Cut pepper in half, remove seeds and pith. Cut flesh in narrow strips. Melt lard, add meat and fry until brown (about 10 minutes). Add onion and pepper, cook gently until onion is transparent. Add plenty of salt and pepper and thyme. Grease a 2 pt (1 l) ovenproof casserole. Put in half meat mixture, half tomatoes, then half spaghetti. Repeat with remaining meat, tomatoes and spaghetti. Sprinkle on cheese and bake.

To prepare in advance: Assemble dish, put in refrigerator for up to 24 hours. Cook and brown as in recipe.

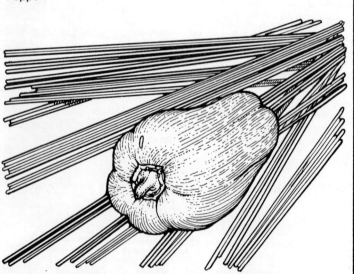

Spaghetti bolognese

Spaghetti is always popular with the young and the very hungry. Made well, it's delicious. Bacon adds to the flavour of the sauce; if you haven't any, use bacon fat for frying the meat and vegetables. You may have the remains of a bacon joint to add instead.

Preparation time: 15 minutes
Cooking time: 30–40 minutes
Serves 4
1 onion
1 carrot
1 stick celery
1 clove garlic (optional)
1 oz (25 g) butter or margarine
2 oz (50 g) diced bacon
8 oz (225 g) freshly minced beef
8 oz (225 g) peeled canned tomatoes
2¼ oz (16 g) can tomato purée
1 bay leaf
¼ pt (125 ml) stock or water
Salt, pepper and sugar
12 oz (325 g) spaghetti
1½ oz (40 g) grated Parmesan cheese for serving

Chop onion, carrot and celery finely; crush garlic if used. Melt the fat, fry vegetables, bacon and garlic gently until golden brown. Add mince, stir and cook until lightly browned. Add tomatoes and juice from the can, purée, bay leaf, stock, salt, pepper and a little sugar. Cook gently, stirring occasionally. Check the seasoning and remove the bay leaf.

Meanwhile cook spaghetti as directed, drain and put on hot serving dish. Pour the sauce into the centre and sprinkle grated cheese over the top or serve separately in a bowl.

To prepare in advance: Make sauce up to 24 hours ahead and put in refrigerator. Cook spaghetti as it is needed.
To freeze: The cooked sauce freezes well.

Macaroni cheese with bacon

Macaroni cheese goes down well for a family lunch in the school holidays. If tomatoes are reasonably cheap, cook some with bacon rolls. Hot bread rolls for really hungry ones would be welcome too.

Preparation time: 15 minutes
Cooking time: 15 minutes
Oven: 425°F, 215°C, gas mark 7
Serves 4

3 oz (75 g) short-cut macaroni
1 oz (25 g) butter or margarine
1 oz (25 g) flour
¾ pt (375 ml) milk
Salt and pepper
4 oz (100 g) cheese, grated
6 rashers streaky bacon

Cook macaroni in boiling, salted water until just tender, according to the directions on the packet (about 10 minutes). Drain and put on one side. Make roux (see page 14) with fat and flour. Cook 1 minute over low heat, stirring. Blend in milk to make smooth sauce. Bring to the boil and simmer 2 minutes, stirring. Remove from heat, add seasoning and most of cheese. Stir in macaroni. Pour into a greased 1½ pt (1 l) shallow, ovenproof dish. Sprinkle with remaining cheese. Derind bacon and cut each rasher in half. Form into rolls and bake with the macaroni until browned.

To prepare in advance: Make, put in dish and sprinkle with cheese. Put in refrigerator for up to 12 hours. Bake in oven to brown bacon rolls.

Baked cheese and potato

Make full use of the oven while this vegetable casserole is cooking by baking some chicken joints or braising some chops to go with the meal. There would also be room for a crumble or fruit to be stewing at the same time. Best cooked and served immediately.

Preparation time: 15 minutes
Cooking time: 50 minutes
Oven: 375°F, 195°C, gas mark 5
Serves 4

1½ lb (675 g) potatoes
½ lb (225 g) tomatoes
1 small onion
Salt and pepper
1 level tbsp flour
5 oz (125 g) cheese
¼ pt (125 ml) water

Peel and slice potatoes and tomatoes. Chop onion. Put potato and tomato slices in layers in a fairly shallow, greased, 1½ pt (1 l) ovenproof dish. Sprinkle each layer with onion, salt, pepper, flour and most of the grated cheese. Finish with a layer of potatoes and sprinkle with remaining cheese. Add water, cover dish and cook until vegetables are tender. Uncover casserole for last 25 minutes to brown cheese on top.

Cheese soufflé

An inexpensive supper dish. To make it a little more substantial, add some finely chopped cooked ham or bacon.

Preparation time: 20 minutes
Cooking time: 35–40 minutes
Oven: 350°F, 175°C, gas mark 4
Serves 4

1½ oz (40 g) butter or margarine
1 oz (25 g) plain flour, sifted
¼ level tsp dry mustard
½ pt (250 ml) milk, scant measure
4 large eggs, separated
6 oz (150 g) strong Cheddar cheese, finely grated
Salt and pepper

Grease a 2 pt (1 l) soufflé dish using butter or margarine wrapping paper. Melt the fat in a pan, stir in flour and mustard and cook for 2–3 minutes. Remove pan from heat and gradually stir in milk. Cook for a further 3 minutes, stirring constantly. Remove pan from heat, beat in egg yolks, cheese and seasoning. Whisk egg whites stiffly and fold into cheese mixture using a metal spoon. Turn mixture into the prepared dish and bake until the soufflé is well risen and golden brown. Serve at once.

To prepare in advance: Make the cheese sauce mixture and add egg yolks up to 24 hours ahead. Fold in beaten egg whites just before baking.

Ham and mushroom omelette

Omelettes make a next-to-instant meal. Check the refrigerator for other ingredients for a change. A Spanish omelette with tomato, pepper, onion and potato makes a more filling omelette, while cold sausage chopped up with a left-over bacon slice makes a tasty change.

Preparation time: 10 minutes
Cooking time: 2–3 minutes
Serves 4

4 oz (100 g) mushrooms
4 oz (100 g) ham
2 oz (50 g) butter or margarine
8 eggs
Salt and pepper

Wash, dry and slice mushrooms. Chop ham. Melt 1 oz (25 g) fat in frying pan. Cook mushrooms for 2 minutes and put on one side with ham. Blend two eggs with salt and pepper using an old dinner fork. Put a 6 in (15 cm) pan on the heat and add the remaining fat, slowly getting it hot and not letting it brown. Without drawing the pan off the heat, pour the egg mixture into the hot fat. It will cover the pan and start cooking at once. Use the metal fork to keep drawing some of the mixture to the middle from the sides of the pan. In 1½–2 minutes your omelette will still be soft but no longer runny. When almost cooked, sprinkle with quarter of mushrooms and ham. Fold in half and turn out on to a hot plate. Serve at once. Repeat with remaining eggs and filling to make three more omelettes.

To prepare in advance: Cook mushrooms and ham a little while ahead. Mix eggs in bowls. Make omelettes not more than 15 minutes ahead and keep hot in a very cool oven, so they don't go on cooking but just keep hot.

Sweet corn scramble

A quick supper dish from the larder shelf. Make sure to drain the corn well otherwise the consistency of the scrambled egg will be too runny. If your family likes peppers, buy the sweetcorn with added chopped peppers.

Preparation time: 5 minutes
Cooking time: 5–10 minutes
Serves 4

6 eggs
6 tbsp milk
Salt and pepper
½ oz (15 g) butter or margarine
7 oz (175 g) can sweetcorn kernels
Toast

Beat eggs in bowl with milk, salt and pepper. Melt fat in pan and make scrambled eggs in usual way. Be careful not to overcook. Just before eggs are ready, stir in drained sweetcorn and cook until hot. Pile on toast and serve at once.

Eggs mornay

Makes a light dish for lunch or supper. Serve with hot rolls or toast, followed by fresh fruit. Best prepared and cooked, then served straight away.

Preparation time: 15 minutes
Cooking time: 10 minutes
Serves 4

6 eggs
3 oz (75 g) Double Gloucester cheese
1 oz (25 g) butter or margarine
1 oz (25 g) flour
½ pt (250 ml) milk
½ level tsp made mustard
Salt and pepper

Boil eggs for only 8 minutes so that they're not completely hard. Cool under running cold water and remove shells carefully. Grate cheese. Melt fat in pan, blend in flour and cook 1 minute. Remove pan from heat and slowly stir in milk. Return to heat and bring to boiling point, stirring constantly. Simmer 2 minutes. Remove pan from heat. Stir in most of cheese, mustard and plenty of seasoning. Cut eggs in half lengthwise. Arrange in ovenproof serving dish. Spoon over sauce and sprinkle with remaining cheese. Brown under grill.

Home-made Scotch eggs

They always taste better home-made. Use fresh sausage meat and add your own fresh or dried herbs. Best eaten on the day of making or the next day.

Preparation time: 15 minutes
Cooking time: 10 minutes
Serves 6

1 oz (25 g) flour
Salt and pepper
6 small hard-boiled eggs
1 lb (500 g) pork sausage meat
$\frac{1}{4}$ level tsp dried thyme
$\frac{1}{4}$ level tsp mixed herbs
1 egg, beaten
Dried breadcrumbs
Oil or fat for frying

Put flour in plastic bag with plenty of seasoning. Shell eggs, then put in bag one at a time. Shake eggs so they are well coated with flour. Mix together sausage meat and herbs and divide into six equal portions. Cover each egg with sausage meat, making sure there are no cracks in meat. Brush with beaten egg and coat with breadcrumbs. Chill in refrigerator before frying. Fry in deep oil or fat until deep golden brown. Drain on kitchen paper.

To prepare in advance: Fry and cook. Keep in refrigerator for up to 24 hours.

Bacon and onion quiche

A perfect combination and just the thing for picnics. You can keep it hot in an insulated bag or box. Failing that, take it hot from the oven and wrap in foil, then a bath towel – and so to the boot of the car. Add grated cheese if you like – matured Cheddar or about 2 oz (50 g) Parmesan.

Preparation time: 20 minutes
Cooking time: 15–20 minutes (pastry); 35 minutes (filling)
Oven: 425°F, 215°C, gas mark 7 (pastry); 350°F, 180°C, gas mark 4 (filling)
Serves 4

Pastry	1 tbsp butter or margarine
4 oz (100 g) plain flour	4 oz (100 g) bacon
1 oz (25 g) butter or margarine	1 egg
1 oz (25 g) lard	Salt and pepper
Water to mix	$\frac{1}{4}$ pt (125 ml) single cream
Filling	or top of milk
2 small onions	

Make shortcrust pastry (see method page 85) and line a 7 in (18 cm) plain flan ring placed on a baking sheet. Chill in refrigerator for 10 minutes. Bake blind (i.e. put dried haricot beans on greaseproof paper to stop shrinking) and remove from oven when cooked. Meanwhile peel and slice onions. Fry in fat until soft but not coloured. Derind bacon, chop roughly and add to pan. Fry onion and bacon until golden brown. Blend egg, seasoning and cream together. Remove baking beans and greaseproof paper or foil from flan case. Put onion and bacon in, straining egg-cream mixture on top. Cook until filling is set.

To prepare in advance: Bake, cool and keep in refrigerator for up to 24 hours. Reheat before serving.
To freeze: Bacon and onion quiche freezes well.

Chapter 8
Rice and vegetables

Salads

Combine celery with apple and walnuts; potato with sliced, raw mushrooms in a lemon mayonnaise; chicory with carrot and orange segments; butter beans with tomatoes; boiled sliced onion with green peppers.

Add segmented orange to carefully stewed apple. Remember that Cox's apples are delicious stewed as well as raw – slightly damaged Cox's are often sold off cheaply in the autumn as they can't be stored.

If your bananas need eating quickly, try baking them with a little butter, brown sugar and orange rind and serve with cream or ice cream.

Add a few cracked apricot kernels to fresh apricots when stewing to give an almond-like flavour, and elderflowers from the hedgerows to flavour gooseberries.

Use the cheaper fruits with the more expensive ones to spin them out: raspberries and cold stewed rhubarb; sliced pears in a purée of blackcurrants; and apples cooked with blackberries.

Nasi goreng

Without doubt this is the best savoury rice dish that I know. The rice ends up a glowing brown colour, beautifully moist and spicy; which comes from the suggestion of curry powder. The recipe is also a good way of using up left-over cold pork or ham, when it will need only about 5 minutes frying instead of the 35 minutes suggested. If you're in a hurry and the family are extra hungry, serve fried egg on top instead of omelette. Best made and served immediately.

Preparation time: 20 minutes
Cooking time: 35 minutes
Serves 4

1 lb (500 g) boned shoulder of pork	6 tbsp soy sauce
	1 level tsp curry powder
½ lb (225 g) onions	Pepper
3 oz (75 g) lard	*Omelette*
3 pt (2 l) water for rice	1 egg
Salt	1 tsp water
8 oz (225 g) refined long-grain rice	Salt and pepper
	Knob butter or margarine
10 oz (275 g) frozen mixed vegetables	4 firm tomatoes

Cut pork into ½ in (1·5 cm) cubes and slice onions into rings. Melt lard in fairly large pan. Add pork and onions and fry quickly for 5 minutes. Reduce heat, cover pan and cook for 30 minutes, stirring frequently.

Meanwhile boil rice in salted water for 10–12 minutes until just tender. Strain into sieve and rinse with hot water, drain. Cook frozen vegetables according to directions on packet. Make omelette. Mix together egg and water. Season with salt and pepper. Melt butter in a small frying pan, pour in mixture and turn when underside is brown. Shred into ¾ in (2 cm) strips.

When pork is tender, stir in soy sauce, curry powder, and rice and mix well. Add vegetables and season well. Arrange mixture in serving dish with omelette strips in a lattice on top and tomato wedges round edge.

Cheese and onion flan

Delicious served hot or cold with a green salad. A good lunch dish – and if left in the tin one of the easiest things to take on a picnic. Cut in slices and eat with the fingers with crisp Cos lettuce or celery. As a change try with the white part of leeks instead of onions.

Preparation time: 20 minutes
Cooking time: 40 minutes
Oven: 425F, 220C, gas mark 7
Serves 6

1 lb (500 g) onions
2 oz (50 g) butter
7½ oz (190 g) frozen puff pastry, thawed
1 tbsp chopped fresh herbs
Salt and black pepper
6–8 slices Cheddar cheese
2 tomatoes; sliced

Peel and thinly slice onions. Fry in butter for 20 minutes, stirring occasionally, and cool.

Meanwhile roll out pastry thinly and line a shallow swiss-roll tin. Drain the onions on kitchen paper towels and arrange over the base of the flan. Sprinkle with herbs and seasoning and cover with cheese. Arrange sliced tomatoes on top. Bake for 20 minutes or until pastry is cooked and the cheese a light golden brown.

To prepare in advance: Make up to 48 hours in advance; warm in moderate oven for 15 minutes to crisp pastry before serving. To freeze: Cheese and onion flan freezes well; reheat as above for serving.

Potato and onion rosti

This is one of the best dishes to come out of Switzerland – one up on our bubble and squeak. To make a complete lunch or supper dish, serve with bacon or fried eggs on top. The potato must be fried slowly so that a thick, golden brown crust is formed on both sides.

Preparation time: 10 minutes
Cooking time: up to 1 hour
Serves 4
1½ lb (675 g) potatoes
1 level tsp salt
⅛ level tsp pepper

3 oz (75 g) butter and margarine, mixed
1 large onion, chopped

Boil potatoes in skins until just tender. Drain, cool and skin; then grate coarsely and add seasoning. Melt 3 tbsp fat in a heavy-based 8 in (20 cm) frying pan. Fry onion slowly until soft. Add potato mixture, press down and fry very gently for 20 minutes or more until pale golden and crisp. Turn potato mixture on to a plate. Heat remaining fat in pan, return potato 'cake' to pan, fried side uppermost. Cook gently for further 10 minutes or more until golden and crisp.

To prepare in advance: Cook potatoes and allow to go cold. Leave in their skins for up to 24 hours. Peel onion.

Summer vegetables au gratin

If your prized home-grown vegetables are not quite a bumper crop yet, combine several to make a meal. A good way to use up odds and ends left in the vegetable rack.

Preparation time: 20 minutes
Cooking time: 25 minutes
Serves 4

8 oz (225 g) new carrots	*Cheese sauce*
½ small cauliflower	1 oz (25 g) butter
4 oz (100 g)	1 oz (25 g) flour
French beans, sliced	¼ pt (125 ml) milk
8 oz (225 g)	¼ pt (125 ml) vegetable water
courgettes, sliced	1 tsp made mustard
1 oz (25 g) fresh	2 oz (50 g) grated cheese
white breadcrumbs	Salt and pepper
2 tbsp oil	
1 oz (25 g) butter	
Salt and pepper	

Cut the carrots into even lengths and cook in a pan of boiling, salted water for 5 minutes. Add the cauliflower, broken into flowerets, and the trimmed leaves and cook a further 5 minutes. Add the sliced courgettes and French beans for a further 3 minutes. While vegetables are cooking, fry breadcrumbs in oil and butter stirring frequently until brown. Season and set on one side to keep warm. Drain vegetables reserving ¼ pt (125 ml) of vegetable water. Dish vegetables and keep warm while you make the sauce.

Make a roux (see page 14) with butter and flour; remove from the heat and stir in milk and vegetable water. Return pan to the heat and bring to the boil. Simmer for 3 minutes and stir in mustard, cheese and seasoning. Pour over the vegetables and sprinkle with breadcrumbs.

To prepare in advance: Only the fried breadcrumbs can be made in advance.

Buttered parsnips

We often mash potatoes with butter and forget that many other vegetables – parsnips, carrots, swedes, turnips, beetroot, celeriac and Jerusalem artichokes – can also be served this way. Any leftovers can be added to soups.

Preparation time: 5 minutes
Cooking time: 30 minutes
Serves 4

1½ lb (700 g) parsnips
Salt and black pepper
1 oz (25 g) butter
1 tsp parsley, chopped

Peel parsnips and cut in half (cut lengthways as well if very thick). Put in cold, salted water and bring to the boil in a covered pan. Cook for 20 minutes or until tender. Drain and then mash well, adding salt, pepper and butter. Beat well with a wooden spoon over the heat. Sprinkle with chopped parsley before serving.

To prepare in advance: Vegetables may be peeled (but not cut up) and kept in cold water for up to 6 hours. The flavour and food value is lost by prolonged soaking or keeping hot for long.

Stuffed peppers

A useful dish for entertaining as it leaves you free with your guests while it cooks. With a loaf of French bread or some soft rolls popped in the oven for the last 5 minutes, no extra vegetables need be served.

Preparation time: 20 minutes
Cooking time: 1 hour 10 minutes
Oven: 350F, 180C; gas mark 4
Serves 6

2 onions	*Cheese sauce*
1 lb (500 g) minced beef	1 oz (25 g) butter
2 oz (50 g) flour	1 oz (25 g) flour
½ pt (250 ml) water	½ pt (250 ml) milk
1 stock cube	½ tsp made mustard
2 carrots, coarsely grated	2 oz (50 g) grated cheese
Salt and pepper	Salt and pepper
3 large green peppers	

Peel and chop onions and fry for 5 minutes with minced beef stirring frequently. Stir in the flour and then water and add the crumbled stock cube, carrots and seasoning. Cover and simmer slowly for 30 minutes. Halve the peppers and remove seeds and white pith. Cook in boiling water for 5 minutes. Drain and set aside.

For cheese sauce, make a roux (see page 14) with butter and flour. Remove from the heat and add the milk, stirring. Return to the heat and boil for 3 minutes. Remove from the heat and stir in mustard, cheese and seasoning. Fill halved peppers with meat mixture, place in a shallow fireproof dish and pour round the cheese sauce. Put in the oven for 25 minutes.

To prepare in advance: Stuff peppers and make sauce up to 24 hours in advance; cover the prepared dish with plastic wrap. Uncover and bake to serve.
To freeze: Stuffed peppers should be frozen before baking.

Savoury rice

Better value than the prepared savoury rice with many variations possible. Paprika can be replaced with curry powder or turmeric, or it can be omitted and the rice flavoured with other herbs. A good way of using up cooked rice and peas or many other cooked vegetables. Left-overs may be moistened with a little French dressing and served cold as a salad.

Preparation time: 10 minutes
Cooking time: 20 minutes
Serves 6

6 oz (150 g) long-grain rice
8 oz (225 g) peas
1 large onion
2 tbsp oil
1 level tsp paprika
1 level tsp dill, dillseed or parsley, chopped
Salt and black pepper

Boil the rice for 12 minutes in plenty of boiling, salted water. Cook the peas, drain both and set on one side. Peel and chop the onion and fry slowly in the oil with the paprika. When soft, but not brown, add the herbs and then fork in the rice and peas. Season. Reheat carefully and serve.

To prepare in advance: Prepare and turn into a covered dish up to 24 hours in advance. Reheat in a moderate oven for 20 minutes.

Chapter 9
Puddings

I like puddings. I like them because they round off a meal, leaving you feeling pleasantly full, and because they can be warming on cold days or refreshing on hot ones.

There are plenty of recipes for traditional puddings, with ingredients ranging from the prosaic to the exotic. Among the cheapest ingredients are windfall apples, which can be served up in a variety of ways or used to eke out more expensive fruits. Soft fruits can be used as a base for all manner of fools, mousses, fillings for pies and pancakes, or added to egg custard to heighten the flavour.

Sometimes it's simply a matter of using a little ingenuity to make a familiar dish with cheaper ingredients. Currant bread in bread-and-butter pudding (page 74), for example, saves buying dried fruit, which is expensive. Almond essence is a cheap substitute for ground almonds in dishes like Bakewell tart (page 77).

Cream makes almost any pudding something special. But cream isn't cheap and it's worth looking around for alternatives. Evaporated or condensed milk can be used to give richness; the flavour can be disguised by adding such things as lemon, rum, coffee or chocolate.

Yogurt is another useful means of enlarging a cream-based pudding. Admittedly yogurt bought in individual cartons is not particularly cheap, but it's cheaper than cream. And if you have a home yogurt-maker, a single carton of commercial yogurt will start you off on pints and pints of the home-made variety. But even without a patent yogurt-maker it's possible to make yogurt at home, using the airing cupboard to provide the gentle heat necessary (see page 80).

Some puddings can be prepared in the oven at the same time as a casserole is cooking — a great saving on fuel. And many puddings need no cooking at all — just some time in the refrigerator.

The recipes that follow cover all sorts of puddings, from those suitable for the most sophisticated dinner party to ones the whole family will demand again and again.

Spiced apple pie

Windfalls are ideal for this pie. The filling is spicy with added raisins, brown sugar, cinnamon and lemon rind. If raisins are difficult to get, or you want to make it cheaper, use chopped dates or any other dried fruit you have in the cupboard. If you are in a hurry, add 2 tbsp of mincemeat instead of adding the spices and raisins.

Preparation time: 20 minutes
Cooking time: 15 minutes + 30 minutes
Oven: 425°F, 215°C, gas mark 7; 350°F, 175°C, gas mark 4
Serves 4

Pastry
8 oz (225 g) plain flour
4 oz (100 g) fat
Water to mix
Filling
1 lb (500 g) cooking apples
2 oz (50 g) seedless raisins
3 oz (75 g) soft brown sugar
1 level tsp ground cinnamon
Grated rind of ½ lemon
Milk for glazing
Icing sugar

Make pastry (see method page 85). Peel, core and slice apples. Chop up raisins. Mix apples, raisins, sugar, cinnamon and lemon rind together. Line an 8 in (20 cm) enamel or tin plate with just under half the pastry. Put in apple filling. Moisten edges of pastry with milk. Use remaining pastry on top of pie. Press edges well down and decorate with a fork. Glaze with milk and make two slits in top. Cook at first temperature and then at second until evenly browned and apple is tender. Serve hot, sprinkled with icing sugar.

To freeze: Once cooked and cooled, freezes well.

French saucer pancakes

A great stand-by for pudding. All the ingredients come from the larder shelf and can be made and cooked in half an hour. Don't use good saucers for making them on, old kitchen ones will do; individual stainless steel dishes would do even better. Take the saucers to table and stand them on ordinary plates. The pancakes will stick like limpets to the saucers, so don't try to turn them out. Make, cook and serve at once.

Preparation time: 10 minutes
Cooking time: 15 minutes
Oven: 350°F, 175°C, gas mark 4
Serves 6

2 oz (50 g) butter or margarine
2 oz (50 g) caster sugar
2 eggs
2 oz (50 g) plain flour
½ pt (125 ml) milk
1 oz (25 g) lard
Jam
Caster sugar

Cream fat and sugar together in a bowl until fluffy. Beat in eggs, a little at a time. Blend in flour. Heat milk until hot but not boiling and stir into mixture. Grease six to eight saucers well with lard and put them in oven until they are hot and the lard has melted. Divide batter between hot saucers. Bake in oven about 15 minutes, or until pancakes are risen and golden brown. Serve at once in saucers with jam and caster sugar.

Hot pineapple pudding

This is not unlike a lemon meringue pie filling and topping except it tastes of pineapple and is cheaper to make. Use the can of pineapple that is the best buy of the day, whether it be crushed titbits or pieces. Best made and served at once. It could well go in the oven at the same time as a casserole is cooking.

Preparation time: 20 minutes
Cooking time: 40 minutes
Oven: 325°F, 160°C, gas mark 3
Serves 4

11 oz (300 g) can pineapple titbits
Water
1 oz (25 g) cornflour
6 oz (150 g) caster sugar
2 eggs, separated

Strain pineapple juice into a measuring jug and make up to $\frac{1}{2}$ pt (250 ml) with water. Put cornflour and 2 oz (50 g) sugar in pan; blend in pineapple juice. Bring to boiling point, stirring. Remove from heat and add pineapple pieces and egg yolks. Turn into a 2 pt (1 l) ovenproof dish. Beat egg whites until they form stiff peaks, then beat in remaining sugar, a teaspoon at a time, beating well after each addition. Spread meringue roughly over pineapple and bake until golden brown.

Lemon and cherry mousse

Marshmallows and cherries give texture and colour to this light fluffy mousse, which should be on the point of setting before these are added. If not, they'll sink to the bottom. Not that it matters very much — some people like to find the nicest things at the bottom.

Preparation time: 20 minutes
Serves 6

Two 6 oz (325 g) cans evaporated milk
1 oz (25 g) glacé cherries
2 oz (50 g) marshmallows
½ lemon jelly tablet
¼ pt (125 ml) very hot water
Juice of ½ lemon
1 oz (25 g) caster sugar
Cream to decorate (optional)

Chill evaporated milk. Chop cherries into small pieces. Cut marsh-mallows into small pieces with wet scissors. Dissolve jelly in the hot water and cool until it is thick but not set. Whip evaporated milk until light and foamy. Add cooled jelly and blend well. Stir in lemon juice, cherries, marshmallow and caster sugar. Turn into individual bowls and chill. Decorate with whipped cream.
To prepare in advance: Chill for up to 24 hours in the refrigerator before serving.

Cream and yogurt brulée

True crème brulée is fearfully expensive to make and quite tricky. This is incredibly easy and is made in 5 minutes. It's worth trying for a special meal when you have little time to spare on the actual day.

Preparation time: 5 minutes
Serves 4

¼ pt (125 ml) double cream
1 pt (500 ml) natural yogurt
Soft dark brown sugar

Whip cream, add yogurt and put in 1½ pt (1 l) glass dish. Sprinkle with ¼ in (0·5 cm) layer of sugar. Put in refrigerator overnight. Sprinkle again with sugar before serving.

To prepare in advance: Always prepare at least 12 hours ahead, then sprinkle a second time with soft brown Barbados sugar.

Apple and cinnamon batter pudding

A batter pudding cooks well under, say, roast pork when the oven is hot. It's best made, cooked and served straight away.

Preparation time: 25 minutes
Cooking time: 20–25 minutes
Oven: 400°F, 200°C, gas mark 6
Serves 6

2 eggs
9 oz (250 g) caster sugar
4 oz (100 g) butter or margarine
Just over $\frac{1}{4}$ pt (125 ml) top of milk
6$\frac{1}{2}$ oz (175 g) plain flour
2 rounded tsp baking powder
1 level tsp cinnamon
3–4 Bramley cooking apples, peeled, cored and sliced

Grease and flour a large meat tin. Whisk eggs and 8 oz (225 g) sugar together until thick and pale. Bring butter and milk to boiling point in a pan then stir into egg mixture. Sift together flour, baking powder and cinnamon, then fold into egg mixture. Pour into prepared tin. Arrange apple slices over batter, sprinkle with remaining sugar and bake. Serve warm, cut in slices, with custard.

Banana cream

The soured cream in this recipe adds to the flavour of the bananas. But you can use yogurt for a sharper flavour.

Preparation time: 10 minutes
Serves 6

1 lb (500 g) bananas
Juice of 1 lemon
10 oz (275 g) soured cream or yogurt
2 oz (50 g) Demerara sugar

Peel and slice all but one of the bananas and blend with lemon juice. Mix with soured cream or yogurt and sugar. Chill in bowl for several hours. Just before serving, pile banana cream mixture into six tall glasses, top with remaining banana, peeled and sliced. Sprinkle with more Demerara sugar.

To prepare in advance: Make up to 24 hours ahead and chill in the refrigerator.

Bread-and-butter pudding

A well-made bread-and-butter pudding is puffed up and crispy on top. A great warmer on cold winter days, especially after a salad or cold main dish. It should not be confused with the stodgy bread pudding made from soaked stale bread and fruit.

Preparation time: 10 minutes
Cooking time: 35–40 minutes
Oven: 350°F, 175°C, gas mark 4
Serves 6

6 large slices currant bread, crusted and buttered
1 large lemon, grated
2 oz (50 g) soft brown sugar
2 eggs
½ pt (125 ml) milk

Cut bread in triangles, arrange in layers with lemon rind and sugar in a 1 pt (0·5 l) ovenproof dish. Blend eggs with milk, pour over bread and leave to soak for at least 30 minutes. Cook until risen and pale golden. Serve at once.

To prepare in advance: Prepare ready for the oven, cover and leave in the refrigerator for up to 24 hours.

Cherry shortbread dessert

A shortbread base is a change from a flan case and is easy to make and very crisp. Any canned pie filling can be used for the topping, but cherry is the nicest. If you want to make your own, use the midsummer cheese cake topping on page 94 and then use fresh fruit in season.

Preparation time: 25 minutes
Cooking time: 20–30 minutes
Oven: 350°F, 175°C, gas mark 4
Serves 4

3 oz (75 g) butter or margarine
1½ oz (40 g) caster sugar
3 oz (75 g) plain flour
1 oz (25 g) custard powder
16 oz (500 g) can cherry pie filling

Beat together fat and sugar until pale. Blend in flour and custard powder, mix to a smooth dough. Roll out mixture to an 8 in (20 cm) circle, place on greased baking tray and prick well with fork. Bake until pale golden. Mark in four wedges with a knife, then leave to cool slightly before transferring to wire rack. When cold, put on serving dish and pile cherry pie mixture on top.

To prepare in advance: Make the shortbread base, cook, wrap in foil or put in a tin until needed. Store up to two weeks.
To freeze: Freeze base for up to three months.

Chilled lemon flan

This is one of the quickest and most delicious flans that I know. The lemons take the sweetness out of the condensed milk, which gives a creamy smooth texture. Top it with any fresh fruit in season: use halved grapes in winter or just a twist of lemon. A tip worth trying is to put the digestive biscuits in a plastic or clean paper bag before crushing. This will prevent the crumbs shooting all over the kitchen table. If you want to make it for six people, make a deeper flan by adding 3 oz (75 g) of rich cream cheese mashed with the juice of another lemon and blended with the condensed milk filling.

Preparation time: 10 minutes
No cooking
Serves 4

Flan case
4 oz (100 g) digestive biscuits
2 oz (50 g) butter or margarine
1 oz (25 g) coarse Demerara sugar
Filling
¼ pt (125 ml) double cream
6 oz (150 g) can condensed milk
2 large lemons
Topping
Any fresh fruit in season, e.g. halved strawberries

Crush digestive biscuits with a rolling pin. Melt fat in pan, add sugar then blend in biscuit crumbs. Mix well. Turn mixture into a 7 in (18 cm) pie plate or flan dish and press into shape round base and sides of plate with back of spoon. Mix together cream and condensed milk. Slowly beat in lemon juice. Pour mixture into flan case and chill for several hours till firm. Just before serving, decorate with fruit of choice.

Chocolate sponge pudding with chocolate sauce

A light, old-fashioned sponge pudding. Thickening the chocolate sauce with custard powder gives it a lovely vanilla flavour.

Preparation time: 20 minutes
Cooking time: 45 minutes
Oven: 350°F, 175°C, gas mark 4
Serves 4

4 oz (100 g) butter or margarine
4 oz (100 g) caster sugar
2 eggs
4 oz (100 g) self-raising flour
½ oz (15 g) cocoa
3 tbsp milk
Sauce
½ pt (250 ml) water
1 oz (25 g) cocoa
1½ oz (40 g) or 1 level tbsp custard powder
2 oz (50 g) granulated sugar

Grease a 1¼ pt (0·75 l) ovenproof dish. Cream together fat and sugar until pale and creamy. Beat in eggs one at a time. Sieve flour and cocoa together. Fold into egg mixture with milk. Turn into prepared dish and bake until well risen and just firm to touch.

Mix 5 tbsp of the water with cocoa and custard powder. Bring remainder of water and sugar to boil. Remove from heat, mix slowly with blended cocoa and custard powder. Return sauce to pan, bring to boil, stirring all the time until thickened.

Gooseberry pancakes

Pancakes make a popular pudding. They may be served with lemon and sugar in the usual way, but they're also very good with fruit. Try them with blackcurrants done in the same way as the gooseberries. Serve with plenty of caster sugar, especially with blackcurrants as they are rather sharp.

Preparation time: 25 minutes
Serves 6

Pancake batter	Salad oil for frying
6 oz (150 g) flour	*Filling*
¼ level tsp salt	1½ lb (675 g) gooseberries
2 eggs	4 oz (100 g) caster sugar
¾ pt (375 ml) milk	2 tbsp water
1 tbsp salad oil for batter	Icing sugar

Sift flour and salt into a bowl. Blend in eggs, then gradually add milk and salad oil, whisking constantly, to make a smooth batter. Make eighteen thin pancakes in 7 in (18 cm) pan; cool on kitchen paper.

Top and tail gooseberries, put in pan with sugar and water. Cover and simmer very gently until they are tender but still retain their shape. Divide gooseberries among pancakes, roll up and place on dish, dust with icing sugar. Can be served with whipped cream.

To prepare in advance: Make pancakes, cool on a teacloth and stack in refrigerator for up to 24 hours. Make gooseberry filling and store for the same time. To reheat, put in filling, roll up pancakes, place in shallow, ovenproof dish, cover with foil and place in oven at 300°F, 150°C, gas mark 2, for about 20 minutes.
To freeze: When cool, interleave pancakes with greaseproof paper, wrap and freeze. Freeze filling separately.

Lemon soufflé pudding

A really different pudding. When it comes out of the oven, the top part of the pudding is soufflé-like with a delicious lemon sauce underneath. If you have a source of cheap cracked eggs, from a market stall for instance, they certainly could be used for this. Best made and eaten straight from the oven.

Preparation time: 20 minutes
Cooking time: 1 hour
Oven: 375°F, 190°C, gas mark 5
Serves 6

4 oz (100 g) butter or margarine	Grated rind of 2 lemons
4 oz (100 g) caster sugar	6 tbsp lemon juice
4 eggs, separated	1 pt (500 ml) milk
4 oz (100 g) self-raising flour	

Grease a shallow 3 pt (1·75 l) ovenproof dish. Beat fat with sugar until smooth. Beat in egg yolks; then stir in flour, lemon rind, lemon juice and milk. Whisk egg whites until they form soft peaks. Fold into lemon mixture. Pour into prepared dish and place in meat tin half-filled with hot water. Bake until golden on top.

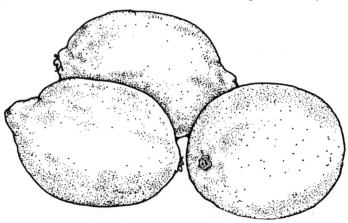

Princess pudding

A variation on the Queen of Puddings theme – an old-fashioned pudding that should not be forgotten. An ideal pudding to have in the oven while roasting lamb for example; it would follow the roast well. For a special occasion, top the pudding with double the amount of meringue, made with two egg whites and 4 oz (100 g) sugar.

Preparation time: 20 minutes
Cooking time: 45–50 minutes
Oven: 350°F, 175°C, gas mark 4
Serves 4

$\frac{1}{2}$ pt (250 ml) milk
$\frac{1}{2}$ oz (15 g) butter or margarine
4 rounded tbsp white breadcrumbs
Grated rind of 1 orange
3 oz (75 g) caster sugar
2 eggs
2 tbsp strawberry jam
Little extra caster sugar

Heat milk and fat until hot. Pour over crumbs. Add orange rind and 1 tbsp of the sugar. Leave 15 minutes to swell breadcrumbs. Separate eggs, mix yolks with crumbs. Turn mixture into a greased, shallow 1 pt (0·5 l) dish and cook until custard has set. Lightly spread with jam. Whisk egg whites until stiff. Whisk in sugar a little at a time. Pile meringue on top of pudding. Dredge with caster sugar and cook until pale golden.

To prepare in advance: Get as far as soaking the crumbs and adding the yolk. Leave in the greased dish for up to 12 hours. An hour or so before serving, put custard to cook and follow recipe.

Bakewell tart

Although it's usual to use ground almonds, I use ground rice and almond essence for this family version. And instead of making one large tart, you can make small ones in patty tins, like maids of honour, for tea.

Preparation time: 20 minutes
Cooking time: 25 minutes
Oven: 400°F, 200°C, gas mark 6
Serves 6

Pastry
6 oz (150 g) flour
3 oz (75 g) margarine
Water to mix
Filling
4 oz (100 g) butter or margarine
4 oz (100 g) caster sugar
4 oz (100 g) ground rice
1 beaten egg
$\frac{1}{2}$ tsp almond essence
2 heaped tbsp raspberry or strawberry jam

Make shortcrust pastry in usual way (see method page 85). Use to line an 8 in (20 cm) plain flan ring placed on a baking sheet. Keep pastry trimmings. Prick base with a fork and leave in a cold place for 10 minutes. Prepare filling. Melt fat in pan, stir in sugar and cook for 1 minute. Add ground rice, egg and essence. Leave to cool slightly. Spread jam in base of flan case. Pour filling into flan case. Roll out pastry trimmings and cut into $\frac{3}{4}$ in (2 cm) wide strips. Arrange in lattice pattern on top of tart. Make them stick with a little milk. Cook until well risen and golden brown. Remove from tin and leave to cool on wire rack.

To prepare in advance: Make up to 12 hours ahead.
To freeze: Bakewell tart freezes well.

Raspberry mousse

Evaporated milk is an excellent base for mousses with a strong flavour, i.e. pineapple, loganberry, raspberry and strawberry. For the best results, chill the can of milk in the refrigerator for at least three hours as it bulks up better when whisked from cold. Chilling the evaporated milk also helps to set the jelly more quickly.

Preparation time: 20 minutes
Serves 4

15 oz (475 g) can raspberries
1 packet raspberry jelly
6 oz (150 g) can evaporated milk
1 tsp lemon juice
2 tbsp double cream, whipped

Strain juice from the raspberries into a measuring jug and make up to $\frac{1}{2}$ pt (250 ml) with water. Put juice in a pan and bring to boiling point. Add jelly in small pieces and stir until dissolved. Leave in a cold place until just beginning to set. Sieve raspberries or put through blender. Put evaporated milk and lemon juice in a bowl and whisk until it forms soft peaks. Fold raspberry purée and evaporated milk into half-set jelly. Mix well, then spoon into a serving dish. Leave in a cool place. Just before serving, decorate with whipped cream and fresh raspberries (optional).

To prepare in advance: Make and chill for up to 48 hours ahead.

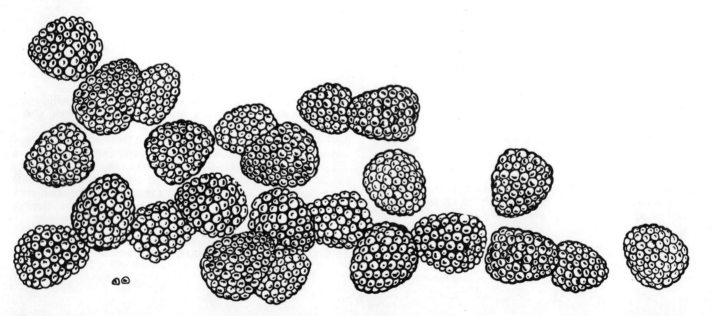

Rhubarb fritters

Apples, rhubarb and bananas are delicious made into fritters. In each case, cut thick slices of the fruit.

Preparation time: 10 minutes
Cooking time: 15 minutes
Serves 4

1 lb (500 g) young rhubarb
Caster sugar
4 oz (100 g) plain flour
1 egg, separated
$\frac{1}{4}$ pt (125 ml) milk
Oil for frying

Sprinkle cut fruit with caster sugar. Sift flour into bowl, making a 'well' in the centre. Blend in egg yolk and then milk to make a smooth batter. Whisk egg white until stiff and fold into batter. Heat oil in pan. Dip fruit in batter, one piece at a time. Fry in deep fat until golden. Drain on kitchen paper and serve at once with sugar and cream — or lemon juice if you don't have a sweet tooth.

To prepare in advance: Make batter up to 24 hours ahead and keep in the refrigerator. Prepare fruit just before frying. Serve as soon as possible after frying, dusted with sugar.

Treacle tart

A classic recipe especially good to have after a salad lunch. Try making smaller individual tarts in patty tins for tea or to take on picnics.

Preparation time: 15 minutes
Cooking time: 30 minutes
Oven: 400°F, 200°C, gas mark 6
Serves 6

Sweet shortcrust pastry
5 oz (125 g) plain flour
1 oz (25 g) butter or margarine
$1\frac{1}{2}$ oz (40 g) lard
1 level tbsp icing sugar
About 5 tsp cold water
Filling
6 rounded tbsp golden syrup
3 oz (75 g) fresh white breadcrumbs
Juice of $\frac{1}{2}$ lemon

Make shortcrust pastry in usual way (see method page 85). Use to line an 8 in (20 cm) fluted flan tin. Heat syrup gently in pan then remove from heat and stir in breadcrumbs and lemon juice. Pour filling into flan case and bake until pastry is golden brown.

To prepare in advance: Make and reheat if the family like it warm.
To freeze: Treacle tart freezes well.

Yogurt

Making your own yogurt at home is an incredible saving since it costs a shade more than the milk itself. It needs little skill and there's no need for special equipment to start with. I make mine in the linen cupboard very satisfactorily! But if you become addicted to yogurt-making, a yogurt-maker will make it in a shorter time and with a slightly firmer set.

Preparation time: 3 minutes
Setting time: 6–12 hours

1 pt (500 ml) milk
2 tbsp dried milk powder
2 heaped tsp bought yogurt

Heat milk to boiling. Cool in a bowl of cold water to about 112°F (45°C)—the temperature of a hot bath. Put yogurt in a bowl and stir. Add milk and whisk in dried milk. Cover, put in linen cupboard or at the back of an Aga cooker for 12 hours, or in a vacuum flask for 6 hours.

Apple and apricot steamed pudding

The addition of apples makes the apricots go a long way, while the breadcrumbs make the pudding light and unstodgy. Dried apricots have a strong flavour so the result is very apricot-ty. Best made and eaten straight away.

Preparation time: 20 minutes
Cooking time: 3 hours
Serves 6

6 oz (150 g) self-raising flour
2 oz (50 g) fresh white breadcrumbs
4 oz (100 g) shredded suet
10 tbsp milk
4 oz (100 g) dried apricots soaked overnight, then drained
1 lb (500 g) cooking apples, peeled and sliced
4 oz (100 g) soft brown sugar

Butter a 2 pt (1 l) pudding basin. Put flour, breadcrumbs and suet in bowl. Add sufficient milk to make a soft dough and divide in three portions, in graded sizes. Roll out smallest portion to line base of basin. Add half of apricots, apples and sugar. Roll second portion of pastry to fit over fruit. Put remaining fruit on top and cover with remaining pastry, rolled to fit. Cover basin with a greased and pleated lid of foil; steam or boil for about 3 hours. Turn out and serve with cream or custard sauce.

Rhubarb crumble slice

Crumble slice is far easier to make than a pie as there is no rolling out of pastry. When cooked, carefully lift out each portion with a palette knife or fish slice. Serve with sugar, essential as the rhubarb will be on the tart side. Also serve custard or cream.

Preparation time: 10 minutes
Cooking time: 40 minutes
Oven: 400°F, 200°C, gas mark 6
Serves 4

8 oz (225 g) plain flour
2 oz (50 g) butter or margarine
2 oz (50 g) lard
1 oz (25 g) soft brown sugar
1 lb (500 g) young rhubarb, sliced
2 oz (50 g) granulated sugar

Make crumble mixture with flour and fats; add soft brown sugar. Use half mixture to line shallow 7 in (18 cm) square tin about $2\frac{1}{2}$ in (6·5 cm) deep. Arrange the rhubarb over crumble and sprinkle with granulated sugar. Top with remaining crumble. Bake until pale golden brown.

To prepare in advance: Make crumble mix and store in plastic or glass-lidded jar for up to three weeks. Prepare rhubarb on the day.

Baby caramel creams

Caramel custard is easy to make, but it's essential to cook the custard slowly so that bubbles don't appear in the custard. If you haven't special dishes use old handleless cups, or make one large one in a $1\frac{1}{2}$ pt (1 l) soufflé dish and cook a little longer. It is also essential to make caramel custard the day before and turn it out on the day of serving, otherwise the caramel will not be absorbed by the custard.

Preparation time: 20 minutes
Cooking time: 2 hours
Oven: 300°F, 150°C, gas mark 2
Serves 4

2 oz (50 g) granulated sugar
4 tbsp water
4 eggs
$1\frac{1}{2}$ oz (40 g) caster sugar
Few drops vanilla essence
1 pt (500 ml) milk

Put the granulated sugar and water in heavy pan. Heat gently until sugar has dissolved, then boil to a caramel. Plunge base of pan in bowl of cold water to prevent caramel burning, then divide caramel among four individual ovenproof dishes.
  Blend together eggs, caster sugar and vanilla essence. Heat milk almost to simmering point and blend with egg mixture. Grease sides of dishes above caramel and strain custard into dishes. Place dishes in meat tin half-filled with hot water. Bake and store.

To prepare in advance: Make the day before, cool, cover and put in the refrigerator for at least 12 hours, then turn out just before serving.

Mincemeat and apple slice

Bought mincemeat is always strongly spiced and is greatly improved by adding apple, either sieved or puréed; it makes the mincemeat go further too. Use windfalls if you have any. The top of the pastry is best glazed with egg white but milk also gives a nice shine if you haven't a surplus egg white.

Preparation time: 15 minutes
Cooking time: 25 minutes
Oven: 400°F, 200°C, gas mark 6
Serves 6

Filling	Pastry case
½ lb (225 g) cooking apples	11 oz (300 g) frozen
1 tbsp water	puff pastry, thawed
Knob butter or margarine	1 egg white
1 oz (25 g) granulated sugar	
4 tbsp mincemeat	

Peel, core and slice apples. Put in pan with water, fat and sugar. Cover pan and simmer until apples are tender. Mash apples to make smooth purée. Put on one side to cool.

Roll out the pastry on floured table to a rectangle 8 in × 12 in (20 cm × 30 cm). Cut into two strips each 4 in × 12 in (10 cm × 30 cm). Lay one strip on a baking tray. Brush round edge with beaten egg white. Stir mincemeat into apple purée, then spoon filling down centre of pastry. Fold second strip in half lengthways. Cut with sharp knife across fold at 2 in (5 cm) intervals leaving 1 in (2·5 cm) of pastry uncut at sides. Unfold strip and place firmly on top of filling. Knock up edges with back of knife and brush top with beaten egg white. Cook until well risen and golden.

To prepare in advance: Cook up to 24 hours ahead and reheat before serving.
To freeze: Freeze before glazing and cooking.

Raspberry boodle

The true flavour of raspberries really comes through in this recipe. For a special occasion add a tablespoon or so of Kirsch.

Preparation time: 15 minutes
Serves 6

15 oz (475 g) can raspberries
16 boudoir biscuits
½ pint (250 ml) double cream, lightly whipped
2 meringues, crushed

Drain raspberries, then sieve the fruit into a bowl with juice. Soak the biscuits in the raspberry liquid for 5 minutes. Mash with a fork, then beat until smooth. Blend in the cream. Pour into a glass serving dish. Chill for at least 2 hours and top with crushed meringue before serving.

To prepare in advance: Make up to 24 hours ahead, cover and chill in refrigerator.

Cider apple compôte

If you have pears available, add as well – the blend improves.

Preparation time: 10 minutes
Cooking time: 45–60 minutes
Oven: 325°F, 160°C, gas mark 3
Serves 4

4 large cooking apples, peeled and sliced
2 oz (50 g) granulated sugar
3 oz (75 g) currants, washed and dried
¼ tsp nutmeg
¼ pt (125 ml) cider

Mix together all the ingredients. Put into a 2 pt (1 l) ovenproof dish, cover and cook. Serve cold with cream or custard.

To prepare in advance: Prepare up to 24 hours ahead, cover and chill in refrigerator.
To freeze: Cider apple compôte freezes well.

Chapter 10
Cakes and biscuits

Making cakes and biscuits is not difficult. I know that there's a kind of mystery attached to the production of feather-light sponges or melt-in-the-mouth pastry. But don't let that worry you.

Start with a recipe in which the ingredients are melted together, like flapjacks, or if they have to be beaten can be beaten by means of an electric whisk. Time spent in creaming the ingredients by hand is time wasted as far as a busy person is concerned.

There is, equally, little virtue in trying to embellish your finished cake with fancy icing. It's much easier — and frankly I think it tastes better — to use the method in which a flavoured icing is poured over the cake while it's still warm and still in its tin. That way, the icing sinks into the cake and gives it a lovely melting flavour.

One of the blessings of cakes and biscuits is that they will keep very well either in the freezer or in a tin. Indeed — if the cakes get as far as the freezer — they can stay there without loss of quality for anything up to six months. It means that you can have a baking day once or twice a month and indulge the family's appetite for weeks at a time.

Shortcrust pastry

Shortcrust pastry is well worth making at home. If you make it up to the rubbed-fat-into-flour stage, without adding the water, you can store it in the refrigerator for several weeks. Use as needed.

Preparation time: 10 minutes

8 oz (225 g) plain flour
$\frac{1}{4}$ tsp salt
2 oz (50 g) lard
2 oz (50 g) cheap butter or cheap margarine
About 2 tbsp cold water

Sieve together flour and salt. Rub in lard and butter or margarine, using the tips of the fingers, until mixture resembles fine breadcrumbs. Bind with water to form a firm dough.

Anzac biscuits

Crisp and crunchy Anzac biscuits come from New Zealand. They spread considerably during cooking, so space them well out on the baking trays. They keep well in a tin.

Preparation time: 10 minutes
Cooking time: 20 minutes
Oven: 325°F, 160°C, gas mark 3
Makes 36

1 heaped tbsp golden syrup
5 oz (125 g) butter or margarine
4 oz (100 g) caster sugar
3 oz (75 g) rolled oats
2 oz (50 g) dessicated coconut
4 oz (100 g) plain flour
2 level tsp bicarbonate of soda
1 tbsp hot water

Grease two large baking trays. Melt syrup, fat and caster sugar in a pan over low heat. Remove from heat and stir in dry ingredients. Dissolve bicarbonate of soda with hot water and add to mixture. Leave to cool for 5 minutes, then divide into thirty-six portions. Roll into balls and place on baking trays. leaving plenty of room between each. Bake until brown. Remove from oven and leave on trays for a few moments to harden. Cool on wire rack.

Weekend fruit cake

Vary the fruit according to what you have in the store cupboard. The cake keeps well — if given the chance.

Preparation time: 25 minutes
Cooking time: 2½ hours
Oven: 300°F, 155°C, gas mark 2

10 oz (275 g) self-raising flour
¼ level tsp salt
8 oz (225 g) butter or margarine
8 oz (225 g) caster or soft brown sugar
Grated rind of 1 orange
5 eggs
1 lb (500 g) currants and sultanas
4 oz (100 g) candied peel
4 oz (100 g) glacé cherries
1 tbsp black treacle

Sift together flour and salt. Cream fat until soft. Add sugar and orange rind; continue to beat until mixture is light and fluffy. Add egg a little at a time, beating well after each addition. Fold in flour alternately with dried fruit, candied peel and cherries. Blend in the treacle. Turn mixture into a lined and greased 8 in (20 cm) cake tin. Cook until a skewer inserted in the centre comes out clean. Remove cake from oven and leave to cool in tin for 10 minutes. Finish cooling on wire rack.

Cheese scones

Use a well-flavoured, mature Cheddar cheese for these scones, adding a little Parmesan for a stronger flavour if liked. As a change, make wheatmeal scones using half plain flour and half wholemeal flour and adding raising agent — 4 level tsp baking powder, leaving the cheese out.

Preparation time: 10 minutes
Cooking time: 15 minutes
Oven: 425°F, 215°C, gas mark 7

8 oz (225 g) self-raising flour
¼ level tsp salt
2 oz (50 g) butter or margarine
3 oz (75 g) Cheddar cheese, finely grated
¼ pt (125 ml) milk and water
Little extra milk

Sift flour and salt into bowl. Cut fat into small pieces. Rub into flour until mixture resembles breadcrumbs. Add cheese and enough milk and water to make a soft dough. Roll out ½ in (1·5 cm) thick and cut into rounds with a 2 in (5 cm) plain cutter. Put on baking tray and brush tops with milk. Cook until well risen and golden brown.

To freeze: Cheese scones freeze well.

Coffee walnut cake

Coffee essence gives a very satisfactory result in cooking, though you may loathe to use it for drinking coffee. Other variations to add to this Victoria Sandwich mixture instead of coffee essence are finely grated rind of orange or lemon. For a chocolate cake use 1 oz (25 g) of cocoa instead of 1 oz (25 g) of the flour (sieve the cocoa and flour together before adding to the creamed mixture).

Preparation time: 25 minutes
Cooking time: 35 minutes
Oven: 350°F, 175°C, gas mark 4

Victoria Sandwich mixture
6 oz (150 g) butter or margarine
6 oz (150 g) caster sugar
3 eggs, beaten
6 oz (150 g) self-raising flour
2 tbsp coffee essence
For filling and icing
4 oz (100 g) butter or margarine
8 oz (225 g) sugar, sifted
2 tbsp coffee essence
2 oz (50 g) walnuts, shelled

Line two 8 in (20 cm) straight-sided sandwich tins with grease-proof paper. Grease base and sides of tins well. Beat fat with caster sugar until pale and fluffy. Beat in egg a little at a time. Fold in flour and coffee essence. Stir just enough to blend thoroughly. Divide mixture between prepared tins. Smooth mixture with knife. Cook until the centres spring back if lightly pressed. Turn out to cool on wire rack.

    To make icing, beat fat until soft; beat in icing sugar and coffee essence. When cakes are cold, sandwich together with half the icing mixture. Spread remaining icing smoothly on top of cake. Rough up with fork and decorate with walnuts.

To freeze: Coffee walnut cake freezes well.

Flapjacks

Some recipes for flapjacks are too dry and too full of oats; this one is more gooey. I always use margarine as the flavour of butter is lost. Flapjacks are ideal for a crowd and keep well.

Preparation time: 10 minutes
Cooking time: 25 minutes
Oven: 325°F, 160°C, gas mark 3
Makes 16

4 oz (100 g) margarine
4 oz (100 g) Demerara sugar
1 level tbsp golden syrup
5 oz (125 g) rolled oats

Grease a 7 in (18 cm) square, shallow tin. Melt margarine in a saucepan, add the sugar and golden syrup and when blended stir in the oats. Mix thoroughly. Press the mixture into the tin and bake. Leave to cool for 10 minutes and then mark into sixteen squares. Leave in the tin until quite cold. Store in an airtight tin.

To freeze: Flapjacks freeze well.

Gingerbread squares

You can eat this gingerbread on the day it's made or put it in a cake tin to mature and get really moist for two weeks before cutting.

Preparation time: 10 minutes
Cooking time: 30 minutes
Oven: 350°F, 175°C, gas mark 4

4 oz (100 g) plain flour
Pinch salt
½ level tsp bicarbonate of soda
1 level tsp ground ginger
1 level tsp ground cinnamon
1½ oz (40 g) margarine
2 oz (50 g) soft brown sugar
2 oz (50 g) treacle
2 oz (50 g) golden syrup
1 egg
3 tbsp milk

Grease and line a 7 in (18 cm) square cake tin. Sift together flour, salt, bicarbonate of soda, ginger and cinnamon. Melt margarine in a pan with sugar, treacle and syrup. Cool until lukewarm. Add egg and milk to pan. Stir into dry ingredients and beat until smooth. Cook until risen and firm. Turn out on to a wire rack to cool. When cold cut into squares.

To freeze: Freeze when cooked.

Lemon ice cake

A beautifully moist cake. The icing (which is just granulated sugar mixed with lemon juice) is brushed over while the cake is still warm and becomes a crisp topping when the cake is cool. Lemon ice cake is quick to make and there's no icing to mop up under the cooling tray as every bit is absorbed by the cake.

Preparation time: 10 minutes
Cooking time: 45–55 minutes
Oven: 350°F, 175°C, gas mark 4

4 oz (100 g) butter or margarine, softened
6 oz (150 g) self-raising flour, sifted
6 oz (150 g) caster sugar
Grated rind of 1 lemon
2 eggs
Icing
4 oz (100 g) granulated sugar
Juice of 1 lemon

Oil a 7 in (18 cm) round cake tin and line base with oiled greaseproof paper. Put all cake ingredients in bowl and beat until smooth. Turn into prepared tin and smooth level. Bake until a skewer inserted in centre comes out clean. Remove from oven but leave in tin.

Mix granulated sugar with lemon juice and brush or spoon over the top of the cake using all the mixture. (The consistency of the icing will vary each time you make the cake according to the size of the lemon.)

To freeze: Lemon ice cake freezes well.

Malt loaf

A well-tried loaf – very popular in our village for cricket teas. You don't need eggs or butter, which makes it inexpensive to make.

Preparation time: 10 minutes
Cooking time: 45 minutes
Oven: 350°F, 175°C, gas mark 4

8 oz (225 g) self-raising flour
1 oz (25 g) Ovaltine
2 oz (50 g) caster sugar
4 oz (100 g) mixed dried fruit or chopped dates
3 oz (75 g) or 3 level tbsp golden syrup
$\frac{1}{4}$ pt (125 ml) milk

Put all the ingredients together in a bowl and blend together to make a thick batter. Turn into a well-greased 2 lb (1 kg) loaf tin and bake until pale golden and shrinking away from the side of the tin. Cool and serve sliced with butter.

To freeze: Malt loaf freezes well.

Open fruit tartlets

Small open tarts are a good way of making fruit go further. When fresh raspberries or strawberries are just coming in season, these tartlets will make the most of just a few of them. If you like, put whipped cream in the base of each tartlet before the fruit. Make and eat on the same day, otherwise the pastry goes soggy.

Preparation time: 20 minutes
Cooking time: 20 minutes
Oven: 400°F, 200°C, gas mark 6
Makes 12

Pastry
6 oz (150 g) flour
3 oz (75 g) butter or margarine
Water to mix
Filling
Selection of fruit, e.g. mandarin oranges, black cherries, grapes
4 level tsp arrowroot
$\frac{1}{2}$ pt (250 ml) fruit juice or water

Grease twelve fluted patty tins 2 in (5 cm) across top. Make shortcrust pastry in usual way (see method page 85). Roll out thinly on floured table. Cut into twelve circles with $2\frac{1}{2}$ in (6 cm) fluted cutter and line patty tins. Prick bases with fork and chill in refrigerator for 15 minutes. Bake blind (put greaseproof paper and dried beans in each tin) for 15 minutes. Remove paper and beans and bake for a further 5 minutes. Cool on wire rack. Arrange fruit in cases. Blend arrowroot with fruit juice or water in pan. Bring to boiling point and simmer for 2 minutes. Cool slightly, then spoon over fruit. Leave to set.

Quick chocolate squares

If your family biscuit tin always ends up with a handful of broken biscuits in the bottom and all the cream or chocolate ones gone, here's a good way of using them up. It's the kind of thing children could make themselves in the holidays.

Preparation time: 10 minutes
No cooking

4 oz (100 g) margarine
2 level tbsp cocoa
1 level tbsp caster sugar
2 level tbsp golden syrup
8 oz (225 g) semi-sweet biscuits, crushed
4 oz (100 g) plain chocolate

Grease a shallow 7 in (18 cm) square tin. Melt margarine in a pan. Add cocoa, sugar and syrup and cook for 1 minute, stirring. Remove from heat and mix in biscuit crumbs. Press into prepared tin. Melt chocolate in a bowl over a pan of hot water. Spread over biscuit mixture and leave in refrigerator to set. Cut into squares when cold.

Sprits

Sprits are one of the most popular biscuits in the Netherlands and they're delicious. If you like, pipe them in rosettes and then when cooked and cooled sandwich them together with butter cream. It's best to use butter throughout this recipe. They keep well in a tin for up to a month.

Preparation time: 20 minutes
Cooking time: 15–20 minutes
Oven: 350°F, 175°C, gas mark 4
Makes 18

1 level tbsp custard powder
6 oz (150 g) plain flour
5 oz (125 g) butter, softened but not oily
3 oz (75 g) caster sugar
1 egg yolk

Sift together custard powder and flour and grease large baking tray. Cream together butter and sugar until light in colour; beat in egg yolk. Stir in custard powder and flour, mix until smooth. Put a large rose piping nozzle in a piping bag and fill with mixture. Pipe on to prepared tray in a close zig-zag pattern about $1\frac{3}{4}$ in (4 cm) wide and three lengths of about 10 in (25 cm). Chill in refrigerator for 30 minutes. Bake until pale golden brown at the edges. While still warm, cut each length into six, and cool on a wire rack.

To freeze: Like all shortbread mixtures sprits freeze well.

Sultana treacle cake

We had this cake often as children and I now make it for my family as a weekend cake. It's beautifully gooey and moist; it also keeps well. Slow baking makes a moister cake.

Preparation time: 20 minutes
Cooking time: 1 hour 25 minutes
Oven: 325°F, 160°C, gas mark 3

6 oz (150 g) butter or margarine
4½ oz (125 g) caster sugar
3 eggs, well beaten
9 oz (225 g) black treacle
6 oz (150 g) self-raising flour
1½ level tsp mixed spice
6 oz (150 g) sultanas
Icing
6 oz (150 g) icing sugar
1 large orange

Well grease an 8 in (20 cm) round cake tin. Beat fat and sugar until pale and fluffy. Beat in egg a little at a time. Stir in treacle, flour, spice and sultanas. Turn into prepared tin. Cook until skewer inserted in centre comes out clean. Turn out and cool on wire rack.

Sift icing sugar into bowl. Add grated rind of orange and blend in enough orange juice to make stiff glacé icing. Pour over top of cold cake, allowing icing to trickle down sides.

Cinnamon fingers

These are a kind of cinnamon shortbread. If you like a more crunchy topping, use crushed sugar lumps instead of granulated sugar.

Preparation time: 10 minutes
Cooking time: 20 minutes
Oven: 350°F, 175°C, gas mark 4
Makes 18 fingers

4 oz (100 g) unsalted butter or margarine
2 oz (50 g) caster sugar
6 oz (150 g) plain flour
½ level tsp ground cinnamon
Beaten egg for glazing
1 level tbsp granulated sugar

Butter a shallow swiss-roll tin. Beat fat and caster sugar together until pale and fluffy. Sift together flour and cinnamon. Blend into beaten mixture. Press into tin and flatten with knife. Brush with a little beaten egg, prick with fork and sprinkle with granulated sugar. Cook until golden brown. Cut into fingers in tin while warm; finish cooling on a wire rack.

To freeze: Cinnamon fingers freeze well.

Honey loaf

Make the loaf using the 'all in together in the bowl' method, then beat for 2–3 minutes (the margarine *must* be very soft and warm). The loaf keeps well – serve buttered in fairly thin slices.

Preparation time: 15 minutes
Cooking time: 1 hour 20 minutes
Oven: 350°F, 175°C, gas mark 4

4 oz (100 g) luxury margarine, softened
10 oz (250 g) self-raising flour
½ level tsp salt
2 oz (50 g) caster sugar
4 oz (100 g) glacé cherries
4 level tbsp clear honey
6 tbsp milk
1 egg
6 sugar lumps, crushed

Grease a 2 lb (1 kg) loaf tin well. Put margarine into large bowl and add flour, salt and caster sugar. Wash cherries in sieve to remove syrup and dry very thoroughly on kitchen paper. Cut in quarters. Add to bowl with honey, milk and egg and beat 2–3 minutes until well mixed. Turn into prepared tin. Sprinkle top with crushed sugar lumps and cook until skewer inserted in centre comes out clean. Cool on wire rack.

To freeze: Honey loaf freezes well.

Orange shortbread

Ring the changes by adding grated lemon instead of orange. Also try using soft brown sugar instead of caster. I've been told that this recipe won a Women's Institute award in Scotland; whether it did or not, it's still beautiful. The cornflour makes it extra short in texture. Butter is a *must*.

Preparation time: 10 minutes
Cooking time: 35 minutes
Oven: 325°F, 160°C, gas mark 3
Makes 12 pieces

4 oz (100 g) plain flour
2 oz (50 g) cornflour
4 oz (100 g) butter
2 oz (50 g) caster sugar
Grated rind of 1 orange
Caster sugar

Sift flour and cornflour together. Cream butter until soft, add caster sugar and continue to beat until mixture is light and fluffy. Add orange rind. Work in flour mixture, adding a tablespoon at a time. Place mixture on baking tin, allowing for slight spreading during cooking, flatten mixture with knuckles to form an 8 in (20 cm) round. Flute edges with fingers and prick shortbread with a fork. Mark into twelve sections with back of a knife and sprinkle with a little caster sugar. Cook until pale golden brown. Leave to cool for a few minutes, then lift on to wire rack to finish cooling.

To freeze: Orange shortbread freezes well.

Swiss roll

A home-made swiss roll is worth making. For a chocolate swiss roll substitute 1 level tbsp cocoa for 1 level tbsp flour. When cooked turn on to sugared paper, cover sponge with a piece of plain greaseproof paper and roll up with paper inside sponge. Leave until cold. Unroll, spread with filling and re-roll. For filling, use freshly whipped double cream or vanilla-flavoured butter cream made with 2 oz (50 g) butter, 4 oz (50 g) sifted icing sugar and $\frac{1}{4}$ tsp vanilla essence.

Preparation time: 25 minutes
Cooking time: 8–10 minutes
Oven: 400°F, 200°C, gas mark 6

Butter
2 large eggs
$2\frac{1}{2}$ oz (60 g) caster sugar
2 oz (50 g) self-raising flour, sieved
3 tbsp warmed jam

Butter a swiss-roll tin and line base with greased greaseproof paper, snipping the paper in the corners. Whisk eggs and 2 oz (50 g) sugar in a bowl over pan of hot, not boiling, water until thick, pale and creamy; then remove bowl from heat and whisk mixture 2 minutes more. Fold in flour then pour mixture into prepared tin, carefully spreading to edges of tin. Bake until sponge springs back when lightly touched. Sift remaining sugar on to a piece of greaseproof paper larger than the swiss-roll tin. Then turn sponge on to sugared paper and peel off the lining paper. Trim crisp edges from sponge and spread with jam. Roll up sponge keeping sugared paper on outside of sponge. Put on wire rack until cool.

To freeze: Swiss roll freezes well.

Cornish saffron cake

Buy powdered saffron (one packet is plenty) from a good chemist; it needs no soaking — just mix with warm water. The cake is best eaten when freshly baked.

Preparation time: 35 minutes
Cooking time: 45 minutes
Oven: 400°F, 200°C, gas mark 6; 375°F, 190°C, gas mark 5

2 oz (50 g) caster sugar
$\frac{1}{4}$ pt (125 ml) hand-hot milk
$1\frac{1}{2}$ level tsp dried yeast
2 tbsp warm water
1 packed dried saffron powder
12 oz (325 g) plain flour
$\frac{1}{4}$ level tsp salt
4 oz (100 g) butter or margarine
2 oz (50 g) raisins
2 oz (50 g) currants
1 oz (25 g) mixed peel

Stir 1 teaspoon of the sugar into milk. Whisk yeast into milk with a fork. Mix saffron powder with the warm water. Leave yeast mixture in warm place for 10 minutes or until frothy. Sift flour and salt into large bowl and rub in fat. Make a well in centre. Pour yeast and saffron mixtures in and beat to soft dough. Put in lightly oiled plastic bag and leave in warm place until double in size. Knead in rest of sugar, fruit and peel, mixing well. Place in well-greased 7 in (17 cm) cake tin. Cover and leave to rise 30–40 minutes in warm place, until risen to the top of the tin. Cook for 15 minutes at first temperature, and until pale golden brown at second. Turn out and cool on wire rack.

Midsummer cheesecake

Vary the topping for this cheesecake according to the season. It could be gooseberries in early summer or blackberry and apple in the late summer.

Preparation time: 20 minutes
Cooking time: 40 minutes
Oven: 350°F, 175°C, gas mark 4
Serves 6

Flan base
4 oz (100 g) digestive biscuits, crushed
1 oz (25 g) caster sugar
2 oz (50 g) melted butter or margarine
Filling
1 lb (500 g) cream cheese
4 oz (100 g) caster sugar
2 eggs
Grated rind and juice of 1 lemon
Decoration
½ lb (225 g) black or red currants
½ lb (225 g) raspberries
3 oz (75 g) caster sugar
4 tbsp water
2 rounded tsp arrowroot

Butter an 8 in (20 cm) spring-form cake tin or ovenproof glass pie dish. Blend together flan base ingredients and press into base of tin. Mash cheese until soft, then beat in sugar, eggs and lemon rind and juice. Turn mixture into cake tin and bake until cake is just set. Leave cake in oven until cold.

Put soft fruit in pan with sugar and water; bring slowly to boiling point and simmer for 2 minutes. Drain fruit, making juice up to ½ pt (250 ml) with water if necessary. Blend juice with arrowroot, return to pan and bring to the boil to thicken. Spoon fruit over cheesecake, then spoon over thickened juice glaze. Remove from spring-form when required but, if you've used a pie dish leave it in.

To prepare in advance: Make and bake. Keep for up to 24 hours in the refrigerator (though it's best made and served on the same day as the flan base can get a little soft).

ALSO AVAILABLE IN THIS SERIES

KNOW YOUR RIGHTS
Dr Michael Winstanley & Ruth Dunkley

This book is a simple guide to your rights in common situations – when buying a house, seeking welfare benefits, or taking legal action, for example.
But getting your rights inolves more than knowing what they are. The authors have therefore included lists of sources of further information – people to see and leaflets to read – to help you with your particular rights problem.
Michael Winstanley – general practitioner, journalist, author and broadcaster – currently presents a citizen's rights programme for Granada Television.
Ruth Dunkley is a social worker with wide experience of interpreting the social services to those in need and to the general public.

CARAVANNING
Barry Williams

One in every seven households in Britain enjoys a caravan holiday at some time during the year and the numbers are growing. If you are thinking of a caravan holiday, or of buying a caravan, this book is essential reading, for in it Barry Williams shows you how to choose a caravan for you and your family. He describes the different kinds of caravans available, the range of accessories and the requirements of the law. He also gives excellent ideas on how you and your family can get the most out of a caravanning holiday.
Illustrated throughout, *Caravanning* is an excellent guide for the beginner.
Barry Williams is Editor of *Camping* magazine and an enthusiastic caravanner.

HOUSE PLANTS MADE EASY
Jean Taylor

This is the practical book for the owner of one or more house plants. Illustrated throughout, the book explains the basic essentials of plant care in clear and concise detail.
The general care of plants is explained – watering, feeding, repotting and propagation – and hints are given on how to make the most attractive use of your plants.
In the second part, 64 photographs of the most popular plants are accompanied by full details of how to care for them.
Jean Taylor is an international demonstrator, teacher and judge and an enthusiastic indoor gardener. She is also well known for her two series on house plants and flower arrangement for Thames Television.

DEAR KATIE
Katie Boyle

Katie Boyle has gathered together hundreds of practical and unusual tips, some of which have appeared in her popular weekly column in *TV Times* over the past five years.
How do you remove spilled paint from a carpet? How can you make the most of your figure? Where do you turn to for help? Katie answers these and many many other questions to make this book an entertaining mixture of information on a great number of subjects.

POWER TOOLS AT HOME
Harold King

Illustrated with nearly 200 pictures and diagrams, this is a book for everyone with modern power tools, attachments and accessories. You can easily tackle many of the jobs in the upkeep of your home and lighten the chores of gardening. You can become an expert woodworker will skill and precision which would otherwise take years to acquire. Harold King is an expert in the Do-It-Yourself field and is the author of a number of books as well as having edited several home improvement magazines.

KNOW YOUR CAR
John Dyson

When the costs of running a car are mounting continuously you need to know how to use your car to its best advantage. Using many illustrations John Dyson in *Know Your Car* explains clearly and concisely how your car works, what can go wrong and what repairs you can easily and safely do yourself.
He also suggests sensible economic driving tips and ways to improve the safety of your car.
John Dyson is a full time author and freelance journalist (has worked on *Drive*, the AA magazine) and has been influential in bringing the problems of car safety to the public's attention.